CREATION
and the
MODERN CHRISTIAN

by
Henry M. Morris

Master Book Publishers
El Cajon, California

1985

CREATION AND THE MODERN CHRISTIAN

Copyright © 1985 Henry M. Morris

Published by
CREATION LIFE PUBLISHERS
MASTER BOOK DIVISION
P.O. Box 1606
El Cajon, California 92022

ISBN 0-89051-111-X
Library of Congress Catalog Card No. 85-060921

Cataloging in Publication Data

COVER PHOTO BY JAMES BLANK

Printed in the United States of America

Contents

Foreword

When the history of Christianity in the twentieth century is written, the name of Henry Morris should have a prominent place for his leadership in promoting the doctrine of creation. His own book, *The Genesis Flood,* (co-authored with John Whitcomb) provided the initial impetus, and his many other books, as well as the many activities of his Institute for Creation Research, have aggressively and credibly advanced the truth of creationism. Not only have Christians been educated, but in many instances the humanistic scientific community has been put on the defensive.

In my own student days, little was said in the classroom about the indefensibility of evolution, and a number of Christians taught theistic evolution, thinking this would satisfy both science and the Bible. Today the scene is totally different. Evolution is openly challenged; demands are being made on school boards to allow creation to be taught in the classroom; national publicity is given to the debate; and even theistic evolution is on the run. No small part of the credit for all of this goes to Dr. Morris and others who, under God, have joined with him.

But still some Christians are complacent about this issue. Thus the burden of this book is to alert believers not only to the errors of evolution but also to the ramifications its teachings have in other areas of life and thought. The revival we need today, says the author, is not from apostasy but from apathy and compromise.

In this book readers will find up-to-date information about evolution presented in a readable and well documented manner. They will hear the author's call to do battle against evolutionary humanism. And they will sense clearly his complete loyalty to the inerrant Word of God. It is a book which will arm all who take the time to read it.

Charles C. Ryrie

Acknowledgments

I wish to express my appreciation to a number of colleagues who have kindly reviewed the manuscript for this book and have offered many helpful suggestions. Most of the latter have been incorporated in the book, but of course I must take final responsibility for its published form. In particular, sincere thanks are expressed to the following:

> John N. Moore, Ed.D., Professor
> Emeritus of Natural Science at
> Michigan State University

> Richard B. Bliss, Ed.D., Chairman of
> Science Education Department, ICR
> Graduate School

> Kenneth B. Cumming, Ph.D., Chairman of
> Biology Department, ICR
> Graduate School

> Charles C. Ryrie, Th.D., Ph.D., Former
> Dean of Graduate Studies, Dallas
> Theological Seminary

Special thanks go to my long-time friend, Charles Ryrie, one of the world's most distinguished Christian writers and teachers. He not only reviewed the manuscript, but graciously consented to write the Foreword.

The manuscript was typed and retyped after corrections and various changes by Mrs. Becky

Nichols. Mr. Tom Manning, Mr. Edmund Liden, Mr. Kenneth Ham and others have reviewed it for clarity and effectiveness from the point of view of Christian laymen who desire that other Christians come to realize the vital urgency of a creationist revival in these critical days. Mr. Ron Hillestad, General Manager of Master Books, has supervised production of the book and made many helpful suggestions.

Henry M. Morris
Institute for Creation Research
May 1985

Introduction

Although there have been many books published on creationism and related subjects in recent years, there does seem to be a real need for at least one more book — a book specifically addressed to Christians and designed with the following goals:

(1) To present to Christians of varied backgrounds the Biblical and theological evidences for special creation, showing that the Word of God clearly teaches the vital importance of literal, factual, fiat, recent creation to their own personal lives.

(2) To alert Christian people to the serious Biblical and theological fallacies and dangers of evolutionism, along with its direct causal relation to the many deadly social, philosophical, economic and religious systems it has spawned and supported. They need to realize that the real root of all the deadly fruits of humanistic thought (communism, abortionism, racism, imperialism, etc.) are in evolutionism.

(3) To confirm to Christians that the real facts of science, correctly and

simply understood, fully refute every theory of evolution[1] and support straightforward Biblical creationism, as well as all other relevant Biblical statements and doctrines.

(4) To prepare Christian men and women for the coming battle between evolutionary humanism and Biblical Christianity, both as prophesied in Scripture and as now quickly assuming fearful proportions in the days just ahead.

(5) To convey the above information in a logical, scientific and well-documented fashion, and also to make it easily understandable as well as challenging and motivating for all true Christians.

The above are ambitious and difficult goals, but these have at least been the writer's aims in *Creation and the Modern Christian*. The reason why a book of this sort is needed is that, despite the revival of creationism that has taken place in recent years, especially among Christians who are professionals in science or other fields of

---

1. By "evolution" is always meant in this book what many have called "macro-evolution," the supposed increase in complexity achieved when a given plant or animal evolves into a higher, more complex kind of organism. The term "micro-evolution" is misleading and is therefore not used in this book since its use is based on the false assumption that micro-evolution (i.e., horizontal variation) can, with time, become macro-evolution (vertically upward variation).

disciplined study, the great majority of Christian people still remain both uninformed and unconcerned.

Whatever may be the reasons for this situation, it needs to be changed. The conflict is real, and will become more serious and extensive as time goes on. In a battle, one does not survive long by professing neutrality and trying to straddle the boundary, unarmed and confused, between the two opposing lines of fire. Elijah's words to the vacillating people of God long ago are even more needed today. "How long halt ye between two opinions? if the Lord be God, follow Him: but if Baal, then follow him" (I Kings 18:21).

I have divided the book into two main parts, each containing three chapters. Part I is mainly non-technical, emphasizing the Biblical and moral importance of creationism, and it is this material that is so vitally important for every Christian in these critical times. These days may well be the last days, so Part I is appropriately entitled "Creation and the Last Days". The issue is urgent and the time is short.

Part II, "Creation and the Witness of True Science", will necessarily be a little technical, but it is essential that all Christians — even those with little direct interest in science as such — realize that true science supports creation rather than evolution. In this scientific age, with the schools and news media continuously asserting that science has discredited the Bible and true creation, an effective Christian life and witness requires that believers be able to answer such claims effectively. These last three chapters provide up-to-date, documented information that will equip any earnest Christian reader with the evidence needed for this purpose.

Forewarned is forearmed, and the modern Christian urgently needs to be prepared for the certain conflict ahead. The writer can only pray that the Lord, in His grace, will use *Creation and the Modern Christian* to that end in many lives.

PART I

CREATION AND THE LAST DAYS

Chapter I

The Biblical Urgency of True Creation

CREATION AS THE FOUNDATION

Creation is a non-negotiable doctrine. What a person believes about origins will surely influence what he or she will believe about meanings and purposes in life. Consequently, in this chapter the critical importance of true creationism will be demonstrated, both from its preeminent place in Scripture and also from its practical place in the Christian life and in Christian history. A brief discussion is also included of the modern creationist revival, with something of its background and its implications for the future.

In Chapter 2, the deadly influences of evolutionism, along with the various forms of humanistic philosophy and practice based on evolution, will be documented. These are not simply academic matters, but are real dangers, wth vital impact in our lives. Christians urgently need to be aware of the real nature and universal influence of evolutionism.

In Chapter 3, the scope and urgent significance of the conflict will be considered, along with the Biblical foreview of its ultimate outcome, as outlined in various key passages on the last days. Then, in Chapters 4, 5, and 6, the scientific evidence will be surveyed, showing (in non-technical fashion) that Biblical creationism is also supported by the real facts of science. Ones does not have to be credulous or foolish to believe the Word of God.

It is high time that people in general, and Bible-believing Christians in particular, recognize the foundational significance of special creation. Creation is not merely a religious doctrine of only peripheral importance, as many people (even many evangelical Christians) seem to assume. Rather, it is the basis of all real science, of true Americanism (as defined in the Constitution and the principles of our founding fathers), and of true Christianity. Evolutionism on the other hand, can be shown to be only a pseudo-science masquerading as science. As such, it has been acclaimed as the so-called "scientific" foundation of atheism, humanism, communism, fascism, imperialism, racism, laissez-faire capitalism, and a variety of cultic, ethnic and so-called liberal religions, especially by the founders and most influential advocates of these various systems. The creation/evolution issue is, in a very real sense, the most fundamental issue of all, representing the only two basic world views — the God-centered philosophy of origins and meanings and that which is man-centered, or theism versus humanism.

FOUNDATION OF GENUINE SCIENCE

Evolutionary assumptions abound in the writings of modern scientists. Leading biologist

Stanley D. Beck says, for example: "No central scientific concept is more firmly established in our thinking, our methods, and our interpretations, than that of evolution" (*Bioscience*, V. 32, Oct. 1982, p. 738).

But it was not always thus. Beck himself, after defining and discussing the basic premises of science (that is, the existence of a real world, the capability of the human mind to understand that world, the principle of cause-and-effect, and the unified nature of the world), admits that "each of these postulates had its origin in, or was consistent with, Christian theology" (*Ibid.*, p. 739). That is, since the world was *created* by a divine Creator, and man was created in God's image, therefore nature makes orderly sense, man is able to understand its operations and true science becomes possible. If the world were merely the chance product of random forces, on the other hand, then our human brains would be meaningless jumbles of matter and electricity and science would become nonsense. Consequently, the great founding fathers of real science (Kepler, Galileo, Pascal, Newton, Boyle, Brewster, Faraday, Linnaeus, Ray, Maxwell, Pasteur, Kelvin, etc.) were almost all creationists and believed they were glorifying God as they probed His works. Yet today such scientists would not even be considered scientists at all, because they believed in the primeval special creation of all things by God!

FOUNDATION OF TRUE AMERICANISM

Although not all of America's great founding fathers were Bible-believing Christians, almost all of them were theists and true creationists, believing that God had created the world and man and

all natural systems. The colonies had been settled
and developed largely by Christian people who
had come to this continent to gain freedom to
believe and do what the Bible taught, and they
acknowledged that the foundation belief was
belief in special creation. The historian Gilman
Ostrander reminds us that: "The American nation
had been founded by intellectuals who had accepted a world view that was based upon Biblical
authority as well as Newtonian science. They had
assumed that God created the earth and all life
upon it at the time of creation and had continued
without change thereafter" (*The Evolutionary
Outlook, 1875-1900,* Marston Press, 1971, p. 1).

Note that these great pioneers were *intellectuals,* not ignorant emotionalists. They laid great
stress on education and science, founding many
schools and colleges, in confidence that true
learning in any field must be Biblically governed.
Christian historian Mary-Elaine Swanson, says:
"In colonial times, the Bible was the primary tool
in the educational process. In fact, according to
Columbia University professor, Dr. Lawrence A.
Cremin, the Bible was 'the single most primary
source for the intellectual history of colonial
America.' From their knowledge of the Bible, a
highly literate, creative people emerged."
(*Mayflower Institute Journal,* August 1983, p. 5.)
In a July 4 address in 1783, Dr. Elias Boudinot,
then president of the Continental Congress,
stated that his reason for advocating an annual
Independence Day observance in America was the
great precedent set by God Himself. "No sooner
had the great Creator of the heavens and the
earth finished his almighty work, and pronounced
all very good, but he set apart (not an anniver-
sary, or one day in a year, but) one day in seven,

for the commemoration of his inimitable power in producing all things out of nothing." (Address to the New Jersey Society of the Cincinnati, July 4, 1783.)

The fact of creation was also clearly implied several times in the Declaration of Independence ("endowed by our Creator," "created equal," "Nature's God," etc.). Marshall Foster has pointed out that at least the first 24 state constitutions recognized Biblical Christianity as the religion of their states (*Mayflower Institute Journal*, August 1983, p. 1).

Yet today, the Bible, Christianity, and creationism have been banned from the schools of the states which had been founded to teach these very truths! All this has been done in the name of a gross distortion of the First Amendment to the Constitution. The amendment which was intended to prevent the establishment of a particular national denomination (e.g., Catholic, Anglican), has instead been so twisted as to establish evolutionary humanism as the quasi-official religion of our public institutions!

FOUNDATION OF TRUE RELIGION

The true religion must necessarily be based on worship of the world's true Creator. Other religions may deify great men, or man-made systems, or the world itself, but these are all merely variant forms of humanism as men "worship and serve the creature, rather than the Creator" (Romans 1:25). It is highly significant that all such religions and religious books begin with the creation, rather than the Creator, *except the Bible!* That is, they all start with the universe already in existence, and then try to delineate how the primeval space/matter/time universe somehow developed into its present array of complex systems. This attribute characterizes both ancient paganism and modern humanism; these and all other atheistic, pantheistic or polytheistic religions are merely various forms of evolutionism. Only in Genesis 1:1 (the foundation of all foundations!) is there a statement of the creation of the universe itself. Without this foundation, true religion is impossible.

Now although creation is the foundation, it is, of course, not the complete structure. Orthodox Judaism and Islam, like Christianity, believe in one eternal Creator, as revealed in Genesis 1:1, but they have rejected Him as Savior. In addition to the general revelation seen in the creation, God has explicitly revealed Himself through both His Word and His Son. Those who reject either or both, even though they believe in one God as primeval Creator and, like Christianity, are monotheistic, cannot know God in His fullness. He must be known in His human incarnation as gracious Redeemer as well as omnipotent, but offended, Creator. Thus, Biblical Christianity is the only truly creationist religion.

FOUNDATION OF CHRISTOLOGY

By the same token, neither can one know Christ as he really is if one knows him only as Redeemer. Faint-hearted Christians often justify their lukewarm attitude toward creation by saying that it is more important merely to "preach Christ." They forget that we are preaching "another Jesus" (II Cor. 11:4) if we do not preach Him as He really is, along with His *complete* work. The threefold aspect of the Person and Work of Jesus Christ is beautifully outlined in the majestic declaration of Colossians 1:16-20.

(1) Past Work, Creation: "By Him, were all things created." Col. 1:16.
(2) Present Work, Conservation: "By Him, all things consist." Col. 1:17.
(3) Future Work, Consummation: "By Him to reconcile all things." Col. 1:20.

The great scope of this threefold work is "all things in heaven and in earth." Jesus Christ was Creator before He became the Sustainer (or Savior) and Reconciler, and the awful price of reconciliation, "the blood of His cross," is the measure of mankind's terrible offense against our Creator. That offense, furthermore, consists essentially of rejecting His Word, and thus denying that He is really the Creator. One truly "preaches Christ" only when he first of all presents Him as the almighty Creator, from whom man was alienated when he repudiated God's veracity in His Word. Only when this is first understood is it really meaningful to speak of God's forgiving grace and saving love, His incarnation and redemptive sacrifice as Son of Man.

FOUNDATION OF FAITH

The great message of Christianity is that "the just shall live by faith" (Hebrews 10:38), speaking of "them that believe, to the saving of the soul" (Hebrews 10:39). But exactly what is this *living* faith — this *saving* faith? Faith in the abstract is only naive sentimentality; it must be faith in something and/or someone to have any substance.

The faith of which the apostle speaks, of course, is outlined in the verses immediately following, the great "Faith Chapter," Hebrews 11. It is the faith of Abel, offering an acceptable

sacrifice; it is Enoch's faith, pleasing God in obedient witness; it is Noah's faith, believing and act-
ing on God's Word; and Abraham's faith, stepping
out on God's promises.

But, *first of all,* it is the foundational faith of
Hebrews 11:3, the faith by which "we understand
that the worlds were framed by the word of God,
so that things which are seen were not made of
things which do appear." This affirmation clearly
tells us that any meaningful faith for salvation
and the Christian life must be founded, first of
all, on faith in God's special creation of all things,
not out of already existing materials but solely by
His omnipotent Word!

FOUNDATION OF THE GOSPEL

Many Christians, who either ignore or compromise the Biblical doctrine of creation, have
urged creationists just to "preach the Gospel —
not creation!" But this is impossible, because the
saving Gospel of the Lord Jesus Christ is squarely
founded on creation. The wonderful threefold
work of Christ (creation, conservation, consummation) as outlined in Colossians 1:16-20, is identified as "the gospel" in Colossians 1:23. The very
last reference to the Gospel in the Bible (Revelation 14:6, 7) calls it the *everlasting* Gospel (thus,
it could never have been any different) and its
message is to "worship Him that made heaven,
and earth, and the sea, and the fountains of
waters."

While it is surely true that the central focus of
the Gospel is on the substitutionary atonement
and victorious bodily resurrection of Christ (I Corinthians 15:1-4), it also includes His coming
kingdom (Matthew 4:23) and His great creation.
Any other gospel is "another gospel" (Galatians

1:6) and is not the true gospel. Without the creation, a supposed gospel would have no foundation; without the promised consummation, it offers no hope; without the cross and empty tomb, it has no saving power. But when we preach the true Gospel, with the complete Person and Work of the Lord Jesus Christ as they really are, we build on a "sure foundation," can promise a "blessed hope," and have available "all power in heaven and earth" through Christ who, in all His fullness, is "with us, even to the end of the world" (Matthew 28:20).

THE CREATION OF THE WORLD AND THE RESURRECTION OF ITS CREATOR

The two greatest events in the history of the cosmos were, first of all, its supernatural creation and, secondly, the resurrection of its Creator from the dead. The evidence for each, to one whose mind and heart are open to evidence, is overwhelming. All real science points to creation, and the best-proved fact of history is the resurrection. The Bible, of course, teaches that both are vitally true, vitally important and vitally related, but even to one who does not believe the Bible; the evidence is still unanswerable. He may reject it, but he cannot refute it.

Furthermore, each is necessary to the other. The creation, invaded and permeated by decay and death, heading down toward ultimate chaos, can only be saved and renewed if death is defeated and life is restored by its Creator. The resurrection, conversely, triumphing over death and promising ultimate restoration of the perfect creation, can only be accomplished by the Creator Himself. The creation requires the resurrection and the resurrection requires the Creator.

It is appropriate, therefore, that the Holy Scriptures so frequently tie together the creation of the world and the resurrection of Jesus Christ. The creation took place on the first day of creation week, and the resurrection likewise took place on the first day of the week following the Creator's substitutionary death for the world's redemption.

Death first entered God's finished creation when Adam sinned (Genesis 2:16-17; 3:17-20; Romans 5:12).

"But now is Christ risen from the dead, and become the first-fruits of them that slept. . . . The last enemy that shall be destroyed is death." (I Corinthians 15:20, 26). Therefore, when the heavens and earth are made new again, the very elements will have been purged of the age-long effects of sin and the curse, decay and disintegration, and "there shall be no more death" (Revelation 21:4; also II Peter 3:10-13; Isaiah 65:17; 66:22; Revelation 21:1; 22:3).

The first book of God's written Word begins with the mighty creation of heaven and earth (Genesis 1:1), but ends with "a coffin in Egypt" (Genesis 50:26). The final book of God's Word introduces Jesus Christ as "the first begotten of the dead" (Revelation 1:5), and ends with "all things made new" (Revelation 21:5).

Let us consider, therefore, three basic aspects of the Christian life which can be greatly strengthened by a clearer understanding and broader application of these two vitally related facts of creation and resurrection. For each, a key passage of Scripture will be found especially illuminating.

CHRISTIAN ASSURANCE

In a society dominated by humanistic unbelief and worldly intimidation, Christians need more than emotionalism to assure them that their Christian faith in the person and work of Jesus Christ not only "works," but is *true*. In the great "Resurrection Chapter," I Corinthians 15, the Apostle Paul is seeking to do just this — to assure these young and somewhat carnal Corinthian believers of the genuine validity of the Christian "gospel" which he had preached to them and which they had believed (verses 1-2). He stresses the key importance of the bodily resurrection of Christ, with the overwhelming eye-witness verification of its historicity (verses 3-11), and then concludes that this guarantees the future resurrection of all who "have hope in Christ," the great promise of the Christian faith (verses 12-19).

But that isn't all. He further emphasizes that Christ's resurrection does far more than provide a future life for individual believers. It restores man's lost estate, reversing the consequences of Adam's primeval sin, conquering all the enemies of God and finally destroying death itself (verses 20-28). This great promise not only gives assurance of eternal life, but strength for a godly life in this present world, triumphing over all opposition and persecution, knowing beyond all doubt there is a better life to come (verses 29-34).

And then, to give still further assurance, he ties it all back to the mighty power of God in creation. All components of the creation (biological — verses 35-39, physical — verses 40-41, and human — verses 42-49) are treated. Every individual creation of God has been designed with its own marvelous structure for its own divine purpose, "as it hath pleased Him" (verse 38). Since each is distinct, none could have "evolved" from any other; therefore only God was capable of creating it, and only He can preserve and revive it. As he raised up Christ from the dead, so will He not only raise, but transform, purify and immortalize our present bodies and the entire travailing creation (verses 50-57; see also Romans 8:18-23). The concluding exhortation, therefore, is to "be steadfast" in our Christian faith and "always abounding" in our Christian work, in absolute assurance that this is *not* "in vain!" (verse 58).

CHRISTIAN REVIVAL

The great need of the Christian church today is revival — not from apostasy, but from apathy and compromise. Apostate churches, denying the basic doctrines of Christianity, are not real churches, but mere socio-religious clubs, and their members still need to be saved. There are multitudes of generally sound churches and believers, however, that have become *neutral* in their stance, whenever they face the controversial issues that require them to choose between conformity to and confrontation with the world system that surrounds them.

Such churches are typified by the church at Laodicea (Revelation 3:14-22), the last of the churches addressed in the seven letters of Revelation 2-3. This church represents a real Christian church, with its candlestick still in place (Revelation 1:20; 2:5), one which seems to be doing well outwardly, in "need of nothing" materially, but one which is "lukewarm," and therefore "wretched" spiritually (verses 15-17). Such churches are urgently in need of revival, not a revival of mere emotional activity, but one of real substance and truth (verse 18) — that is, *repentance* (verse 19).

It is significant that the Lord Jesus Christ, in addressing the Laodicean church, begins with an emphasis on the creation and ends with the resurrection and promised consummation. These are the most fundamental of all doctrines, consequently the ones most resisted by the world, and thus the doctrines on which there is the greatest temptation to become "lukewarm." The Lord calls such churches first of all to recognize Him as the "Amen, the faithful and true witness, the beginning of the creation of God" (verse 14). He concludes by reminding them that His resurrection and ascension provide the only assurance of their own future resurrection for the coming kingdom. "To him that over-cometh will I grant to sit with me in my throne, even as I also overcame, and am set down with my Father in His throne" (verse 21). How urgent is it for churches today, with all their emphasis on self-centered spirituality and so-called abundant living, to get back to an understanding and proclamation of the bedrock doctrines of creation and resurrection.

CHRISTIAN WITNESS

When a Christian has firm assurance of his own salvation and is properly motivated in terms of God's eternal purposes, then it is his responsibility to bear witness to others who need this great salvation, wherever and by whatever means he can, as God leads and enables.

No doubt the greatest Christian witness was the Apostle Paul, and his example surely deserves study and emulation. It is significant that Paul always began where his listeners already were, in their own prior understanding of God and His pur-

poses. When they already knew and believed the
Old Testament Scriptures, he would show them
from the Scriptures that Christ was the promised
Messiah, going on from there to the resurrection
as the conclusive proof. When, however, his
listeners neither knew nor believed the Scriptures,
he would start with the evidence of God in creation, which they had distorted into a pantheistic
polytheism. The classic example is that of the
Greek philosophers at Athens (Acts 17:15-34).
Note his words:

> "Whom therefore ye ignorantly wor-
> ship, Him declare I unto you. God
> that made the world and all things
> therein, seeing that He is Lord of
> heaven and earth,. . . giveth to all
> life, and breath, and all things"
> (verses 23-25).

Then, in anticipation of the natural question as
to how one would know which of the "gods" was
really the God who had created all things, the
Apostle first had to point out that the Creator of
all men must also be the Judge of all men, and
that all men needed to repent and turn back to
Him.

> "Because He hath appointed a day,
> in the which He will judge the world
> in righteousness by that man whom
> He hath ordained; whereof He hath
> given assurance unto all men, in
> that He hath raised Him from the
> dead" (verse 31).

This two-fold testimony — creation pointing to
the fact of God and the resurrection identifying
the person of God — constitutes an irrefutable

witness, so that God can in perfect equity on this basis, "command all men everywhere to repent" (verse 30). Even though death triumphs over all other men, it could never defeat the Creator of life, and no one who believes in creation should ever stumble at the resurrection. As Paul challenged King Agrippa, "Why should it be thought a thing incredible with you, that God should raise the dead?" (Acts 26:8)

By the same token, one who accepts the factuality of Christ's resurrection should never stumble over God's record of creation. Yet there seem to be multitudes of compromising Christians today who are willing to believe that Christ was raised from the dead but who still reject His testimony about creation. "From the beginning of the creation God made them male and female," He said (Mark 10:6, referring to Genesis 1:27). Not after 18 billion years of cosmic history and 4.5 billion years of earth history, but *from the beginning of the creation,* God made man and woman. In fact, the very purpose of the earth's creation was that it should be a home for "the children of men" (Psalm 115:16). How can a Christian believe Christ's words and then reject Moses' words?

> "For had ye believed Moses, ye would have believed me: for he wrote of me. But if ye believe not his writings, how shall ye believe my words?" (John 5:46,47).

The Lord Jesus said, in two of the great "I am" passages of the book of Revelation:

> "I am Alpha and Omega, the beginning and the ending, . . . which is,

and which was, and which is to
come, the Almighty" (Revelation
1:8).

And then he also said:

"I am He that liveth, and was dead;
and, behold, I am alive forevermore.
Amen; and have the keys of hell and
of death" (Revelation 1:18).

He is both "before all things" and the "firstborn
from the dead" (Colossians 1:17, 18). Therefore,
He is "able to save them to the uttermost that
comes unto God by Him" (Hebrews 7:25).

CREATION AND THE COMING OF CHRIST

The great mystery of the Incarnation can never
be fully understood by mortals, but it is the
absolutely indispensable object of our faith.
According to both Scripture and science, the fact
of creation is the foundation of all truth and life,
but "no man hath seen God at any time" (John
1:18). How the great Creator could Himself enter
human life and become the Savior of His creation
is impossible for finite human minds to
comprehend, but the fact that He *did* come into
the world as the very Son of Man, dying to take
away the sin of the world, is the central truth and
focus of history. Furthermore, the fact of His
resurrection makes it equally certain and vital
that He come into the world again, not again for
suffering and sacrifice but in judgment and
triumph.

Thus the Creator who has become Savior will
also be Consummator and eternal Sovereign.

"Unto them that look for Him shall He appear the second time without sin unto salvation" (Hebrews 9:28). The coming of the Creator into the world — both for His human incarnation and for His final, everlasting reign — comprises all the motivation and power for Christian faith and life. But to understand the meaning of His coming, one must first understand and believe the record of His primeval work of creation and man's terrible rebellion against Him.

THE FIRST COMING OF THE CREATOR

At Creation, the Lord looked forward to the Incarnation. At the Incarnation, He had to anticipate the Cross. Then, on the Cross, He looked beyond to the Crown! The eternal Word, by whom all things were made, was Himself made flesh (John 1:1-3, 14), when He came into the world He had made. Thus did creation foretell Christmas, and Christmas fulfill creation.

The word "Christmas," in its primary sense, means "Christ-Sent," or "Christ's Mission" (the suffix *mas* is derived ultimately from the Latin *mittere*, "to send"). He came as God's greatest Missionary, manifesting the love of God toward us, "because that God sent His only begotten Son into the world, that we might live through Him" (I John 4:9).

But this required the Cross, and so He "became obedient unto death, even the death of the cross" (Philippians 2:8). Nevertheless, He, "for the joy that was set before Him endured the cross, despising the shame" (Hebrews 12:2), and therefore He will someday be crowned King of kings and Lord of lords.

One of the most poignantly sad verses in all the Bible is John 1:10. "He was in the world, and the world was made by Him, and the world knew Him not." How could it possibly be that men and women, lovingly formed and commissioned by their Maker to enjoy productive and happy lives in a world of beauty and fullness, could then turn on Him and refuse His loving guidance?

Yet that is what Adam and Eve did even though they had walked with Him and talked with Him in the beautiful garden He had planted for them. Worse yet, that is what the whole world did when God the Creator eventually came into the world again, this time only to be despised and crucified by the ones He loved. But, of course, those were cruel days, when people were still brutish and ignorant, caring little for the grace of life, steeped in the carnality of pagan religion and unaware of their long-forgotten Maker. If only He had waited until the twentieth century to come into the world, when the marvels of modern science and communication, culture and education, would have spread the joyful news quickly all over the world!

But then as one takes a closer look at the pseudo-intellectual arrogance of the establishment scientists, the skeptical bias of the communications media, the depravity of modern pseudo-intellectual humanistic culture and the anti-creationist mindset of the educators, it becomes obvious that Christ would be even more rapidly and cruelly repudiated in the modern world then He was in the ancient world.

As a matter of fact, He *will* be coming again one day into the world that was made by Him, and the world will indeed know Him this time — not as a loving Savior but as an offended and angry Creator and Judge! "God that made the world and all things therein ... hath appointed a

day, in the which He will judge the world in
righteousness by that man whom He hath ordained; whereof He hath given assurance unto all
men, in that he hath raised Him from the dead"
(Acts 17:24, 31).

Until He comes again, however, this is still the
age of grace and there is still the wonderful
Christmas message of salvation to all who will
hear. The great Creator has become the incarnate
Word, and the Savior of men. "He came unto His
own, and His own received Him not. But as many
as received Him, to them gave He power to
become the sons of God, even to them that
believe on His name" (John 1:11, 12).

Christmas is thus only one stage, a preparatory
stage, in God's great plan of the ages. Yet it is
the only one which the world as a whole acknowledges. Creation is denied, the Cross is ignored,
and the Coronation is ridiculed; but Christmas is
eulogized, commercialized, and scandalized. It
often seems as though human activities for the
first 51 weeks of each year are designed merely
to support a year-end madness of covetousness
and revelry in its final week.

But there is much *beyond* Christmas! For the
Lord Jesus, there was a lifetime of service and
sacrifice, consummated by eternal joy. "As my
Father hath sent me, even so send I you," He
said. For us also, as His servants, there must be
service and sacrifice and, then, ultimately
satisfaction and joy everlasting.

THE LAST COMING AND THE NEW CREATION

At Christmas, the Christian world rejoices in
the glorious fact of the first coming of Christ,
when "the Word was made flesh and dwelt (literally
"tabernacled") among us" (John 1:14), and men

"beheld His glory."

But His tabernacling was only for a little while. He came down from heaven, and heaven was on earth, but earth would not receive her King, and the glory departed. "He that descended is the same also that ascended up far above all heavens, that He might fill all things" (Ephesians 4:9).

The earth would not receive Him, but it was made by Him and His people long for Him. "For the earnest expectation of the creation waiteth for the manifestation of the sons of God' (Romans 8:19).

Therefore, there will be a second coming of Christ! "For the Lord himself shall descend from heaven with a shout, with the voice of the archangel, and with the trump of God: and the dead in Christ shall rise first: Then we which are alive and remain shall be caught up together with them in the clouds, to meet the Lord in the air: and so shall we ever be with the Lord" (I Thessalonians 4:16, 17).

But even that is not enough, and the earth will continue yet many a year in travail, groaning in pain to be delivered. The nations in the four quarters of the earth must gather to battle against God one time more. He came down to them out of heaven first in grace and patience, but this time will it be said that "fire came down from God out of heaven, and devoured them" (Revelation 20:9).

Finally there will be a *third* coming of Christ — a *last* coming of Christ, this time with His Holy City — to the earth, made new in its fiery cleansing and ready to serve eternally as the home of the glorified Christ, with all his saints.

"Behold, the tabernacle of God is with men, and

He will dwell with them" (Revelation 21:3). This time His tabernacling among us will be forever, and His glory our unending light. We shall dwell with Him and serve Him in Immanuel's land, world without end.

Does such a prospect seem unreal and far away? Just as His first coming was real, and His second coming is soon, so His last coming is sure! "Which hope we have as an anchor of the soul, both sure and steadfast" (Hebrew 6:19).

That is the *real* world — the eternal world — for which we must prepare in this present world. As we look back to His first coming, we must also look forward to His final coming, for "when Christ, who is our life, shall appear, then shall ye also appear with Him in glory" (Colossians 3:4).

THE CREATIONIST TESTIMONY IN HEAVEN

An amazing scene appears before our eyes in the fourth chapter of the Book of Revelation. The throne of God is unveiled in the heavens and around the throne appear four wonderful and mysterious beings. Because the Greek term is *zoon* (a word from which we derive such words as "zoology"), the King James translators simply called them "beasts"; other versions call them "living ones." Their respective appearances are said to be those of a lion, a calf, a man and an eagle (Revelation 4:7) and this fact identifies them with the four mighty cherubim of Ezekiel 1:10 and 10:14.

Whenever these remarkable creatures are mentioned in the Bible, they are closely associated with the personal presence of God in His glory. But first of all they are encountered at the gates of Eden, with flaming swords keeping the way of the tree of life after the expulsion of Adam and

Eve (Genesis 3:24) from the garden.

These are the highest creatures in all the angelic host of heaven. Once there were apparently five cherubim and the highest of all, the "anointed cherub that covereth" (Ezekiel 28:14) was none other than Satan himself. Until iniquity was found in him this "covering cherub" had been perfect in all his ways. When he rebelled, he was "cast to the earth" (Ezekiel 28:15-17). After his fall, though his ultimate doom was assured, his created eminence was still so exalted that even Michael the archangel dared not rebuke him directly (Jude 9). Thus the yet *unfallen* cherubim must be indescribably lofty and majestic!

It is these highest beings among all the heavenly "principalities and powers," created originally by the eternal Son of God (Colossians 1:16) whom the Apostle John saw in his great vision of the last days. There, around the throne in the heavens, John heard a great testimony of thanksgiving and praise, led by none other than the cherubim themselves!

"And when those (Cherubim) give glory and honor and thanks to Him that sat on the throne, . . . the four and twenty elders fall down before Him . . . saying, Thou art worthy, O Lord, to receive glory and honor and power: for thou hast created all things, and for thy pleasure they are and were created" (Revelation 4:9-11).

Whether or not the twenty-four elders represent all the redeemed men and women who will be in heaven, as most expositors believe, it is fitting for us even today to practice this great testimony of thanksgiving, anticipating the sure day to come when we appear in His presence, where the cherubim dwell, and where they also give thanks to God. If the highest angels worship and rejoice as they thank God for His great creation, so should we.

Then, one day, when God's great curse on the creation, first occasioned because of the rebellious cherub, is finally removed forever, the four faithful cherubim will swing open the gates of Eden once more, and there will be free access eternally to the tree of life (Revelation 2:7, 22:1-4) and to the presence of our Savior. And so, "Know ye that the Lord He is God: it is He that hath made us, and not we ourselves; we are His people, and the sheep of His pasture. Enter into His gates with thanksgiving, and into His courts with praise: be thankful unto Him, and bless His name. For the Lord is good; His mercy is everlasting: and His truth endureth to all generations" (Psalm 100:4, 5).

THE MODERN REVIVAL OF THE DOCTRINE OF CREATION

It is strange and sad that we have to speak of a "revival" of creationism. As just pointed out, the doctrine of creation is foundational to every other doctrine of Christianity, and a practical awareness of its significance is vital to the Christian life. Thus, its century-long eclipse is bound to be the underlying cause of the modern widespread indifference to Christian truth and righteousness. In any case, the refreshing winds of creationist revival have indeed been blowing across the world in recent years, and there is probably no development of modern times which is more significant than this. Despite a hundred years of evolutionist indoctrination in the schools and colleges, recent polls have shown that a majority of the American people have returned to a belief in special creation, with almost half the population even believing in *recent* creation, just as the Bible teaches.

This development has taken the scientific and educational establishments quite by surprise, and they are now reacting angrily and vigorously. Consequently, even Christians who would prefer not to be involved in the creation/evolution controversy are sooner or later going to have to take part one way or another. The evolutionists will never allow neutrality, so Christians need at least to become informed before they make their choice. In this section will be given a brief historical review of the creation movement and then a very brief survey of the two competing "models" of origins. For more extensive background and orientation, see my book, *History of Modern Creationism* (published by Master Books, 1984, 384 pp.).

HISTORICAL BACKGROUND

The factors that initiated the resurgence of creationism are varied and it is necessary to oversimplify for the sake of brevity. A number of historians who have tried to trace these developments, however, have said that the major catalyst which triggered the accumulated ingredients into action was the publication of a certain book a little more than 20 years ago: *The Genesis Flood* by John C. Whitcomb and Henry M. Morris (Presbyterian and Reformed Publishing Co., 1961, 518 pages). To date this book has gone through over 30 printings in America. It has also been published in a British edition, and in German and Spanish translations. Its unique co-authorship by a theologian and scientist, together with its attempt at a fully documented exposition of the relevant Biblical and scientific data — especially the geological data bearing on earth "history" — in the context of a recent six-day creation and subsequent worldwide flood, seemed to be what many were waiting for, and it soon generated wide attention, both for and against.

Many hitherto silent creationists began to become vocal, and many theistic evolutionists were converted to creationism. I have received large numbers of unsolicited testimonies of people who became converts, not only to creationism but even to Christianity (although the book was not written in any sense as an evangelistic tract) through reading *The Genesis Flood*. Even though it has long needed updating (the case for creationism is much stronger now!) it is still selling as well as ever. On the other hand, most evolutionists (even most theistic evolutionists) reacted violently against it and still do.

An important development largely catalysed by *The Genesis Flood* was the formation of the Creation Research Society in 1963. Initially started as a "creation research committee" of ten men, it quickly grew to eighteen, with these eighteen men (most of whom had read *The Genesis Flood* manuscript while it was being prepared for publication) becoming the first Board of Directors. A statement of faith was adopted, along with a constitution which assured the permanency of its statement of faith and continuing control by its founding members. Dr. Walter Lammerts, prize-winning horticultural geneticist, was the first president, followed at approximate five-year intervals by Henry Morris, physicist Tom Barnes, botanist George Howe, and biologist Wilbert Rusch. A quarterly journal of significant research papers in scientific and Biblical creationism was initiated, and has continued to the present. The Society membership grew quickly and now includes approximately 700 voting members (all of whom have post-graduate degrees in some field of natural science) plus about 2,000 sustaining members, all subscribing to its strongly creationist and Biblical statement of faith.

Since that time, many other creationist societies have been formed, both local and national, and in many countries. All are membership organizations, some with a strong scientific emphasis but most with a more popular and often political thrust, attempting to promote or even to legislate the reintroduction of creationism into schools and other public institutions.

However, the organization generally credited with the greatest impact towards the modern creationist revival is not a society but an actual institution, with a full-time staff of scientists and support personnel. First established in 1970, it has been known as the Institute for Creation Research since 1972. I became its founder, leaving a 30-year career in secular education to help found a creationist liberal arts college (Christian Heritage College in San Diego) along with ICR in 1970. The Institute and its activities are discussed more fully on pages 32-35.

THE CASE FOR CREATION OUTLINED

As far as the case for creation[1] is concerned, there are both religious and scientific dimensions

---

1. The scientific case for creation, outlined in this section, is discussed more fully in Chapters 4, 5, and 6.

involved. The Bible clearly teaches special creation and so did Jesus Christ, so that Bible-
believing Christians naturally tend to become
committed creationists. Furthermore, the various
anti-Christian systems historically based on some
form of evolutionary philosophy (humanism,
atheism, fascism, racism, communism,
existentialism, social Darwinism, etc.) as well as
the logical difficulty involved in trying to
attribute the evolutionary process — with its
waste and randomness and cruelty — to a God of
wisdom and power and love, combine to make it
completely inconsistent for a real theist to accept
evolution except on the basis of personal
expediency.

But the scientific case for creation is as definite
and clear as the religious case and can, in fact,
be developed quite independently of the religious
case. Herein is the real basis for the great success of modern creationism. The debate in the
last two decades, unlike that in earlier times, has
focused mainly on the scientific data. Creationists point out that neither creation nor evolution can be *proved* or even really tested, since
both are in the realm of history, outside the
scope of the scientific method. Nevertheless, they
maintain that the "creation model" can be used
to explain the observed scientific data far better
than the "evolution model."

In some cases of course, the two models will
"predict" the same things, and therefore data of
this sort cannot provide any basis for deciding
between the models. Both creationists and evolutionists, for example, would expect to see rapid
"horizontal" variation within each "kind" of
organism, enabling it to adjust through natural
selection to changing environments. Similarly,

proponents of both models would predict more or
less parallel similarities in genetic chemistry, embryology and morphology, one on the basis of
common design, the other on the basis of
common descent.

However, the evolutionist should expect to see
unlimited variation, with small horizontal
changes eventually becoming big "vertical"
changes, and he should expect to see an evolutionary *continuum* of organisms, since all supposedly evolved from a common ancestor in the
same world by the same process. The creationist,
on the other hand, predicts limited change only,
with clearcut gaps between kinds, and differences
as well as similarities. The evolution model can,
of course, be expanded to accommodate these
difficulties, but the creation model *fits the facts
directly!* Furthermore, since evolution is supposedly still going on, the evolutionist must suppose some basic "law of innovation and integration" to exist in nature, somehow bringing complex systems into being and then building them
up into higher levels of complexity. This law or
process ought to be observable, since it
presumably is still operating. In the past it supposedly has produced a cosmos from primeval
chaos, life from non-life, higher kinds from lower
kinds, and man from the beast.

The creationist, however, predicts the exact
converse of this. He predicts a basic principle of
conservation and disintegration in nature with
the created systems *conserved* quantitatively in
their created essence, while *disintegrating*
qualitatively from their created state of
primeval perfection.

Now it is remarkable that the two most basic
and certain laws of nature are the laws of

conservation and disintegration — conservation of quantity and disintegration of quality. In the physical sciences these principles are recognized as the famous First and Second Laws of Thermodynamics. They conform explicitly to the "expectations" of the creation model, but they obviously contradict the evolution model. In the biological sciences they can be recognized as the law of biogenesis ("like begets like") and the universally harmful nature of mutations, as well as the phenomena of aging, atrophy, death and extinction.

It may be — someday — the evolution model can be modified sufficiently to accommodate these basic laws of science (though evolutionists have not yet been able to do it and many of them don't even seem to understand the problem). Even if that should happen, it still won't be as good as the creation model, which *"predicts"* the laws!

But the key test is that of history, which presumably is recorded for us in the fossil evidence in the sedimentary rocks of the earth. If the evolution model is correct, then the fossils ought to record that history, showing the gradual evolution of all forms of life from their common ancestor. There ought to be a multitude of transitional forms in the fossil record — in fact they should *all* be transitional forms!

The creationist, on the other hand, expects to find *no* transitional forms. He expects to find essentially the same situation as in the present world — that is, much variation within kinds but clear-cut gaps between kinds, with also much evidence of atrophy and extinction. And what is the actual case in the fossils? The fossil record confirms explicitly the predictions of the creationist.

The fossils do not include *any* transitional forms. There are variations within kinds (e.g., the horses) and kinds which are "mosaics" of structural features of various kinds (e.g., the duck-billed platypus, which has a curious combination of features associated usually with reptiles, birds and mammals) but there are no animals, either living or fossil, which possess transitional evolving structures (e.g., scales turning into feathers, legs becoming wings).

This complete absence of any incipient or transitional structures, out of the hundreds of millions of documented fossils, has become so notorious that even evolutionists are now acknowledging that the fossil record gives no evidence for evolution. See, for example, "Who Doubts Evolution?" by the Oxford University zoologist, Mark Ridley, (*American Biology Teacher*, V. 90, June 25, 1981, p. 831). It has led many of the new school of paleontologists to adopt the Marxist system of "revolutionary evolutionism" or "punctuated equilibrium." This system abandons Darwinian gradualism in favor of the concept of long stable periods of "stasis" interrupted by occasional spurts of rapid evolution in small populations (undocumented by any transitional fossils, of course).

This strange theory (also called the "hopeful monster" theory) has no genetic basis, no thermodynamic basis, and no positive evidence of any kind whatever. It is based explicitly on the *absence* of evidence! Its sole merits seem to be that it fits in nicely with the Marxist philosophy of many of its leading advocates and, even more importantly, provides an excuse to continue to reject the tremendous creationist testimony of the fossil record. The fossil record not only speaks clearly of creation, but also of universal catastrophism. Like evolutionary gradualism, geological uniformitarianism is also suffering from lack of evidence. More and more geologists (e.g., Derek Ager: *The Nature of the Stratigraphic Record* (New York, John Wiley, 1981, 114 pages) are recognizing that all geological formations and structures must be explained, not by the slow processes of the present (uniformitarianism), but by intense catastrophic phenomena of the past. Furthermore, it is known that there is no worldwide geologic "unconformity" (or time gap) recorded in the geologic column of sedimentary rock beds everywhere, which means that the depositional process which laid down the rock-forming materials, was continuous, with no worldwide time gap between successive formations or successive "ages." That being the case, since every formation was deposited rapidly, the whole geologic column was formed rapidly — in a global hydraulic cataclysm! This in turn means that the fossil record does not record the evolution of life over many ages, but the destruction of life in one age.

The fossil "zones" are not "ages" but rather ecological communities, with those in habitats of lower elevation buried most deeply. It is not surprising to the creationist, therefore (though it should be to the evolutionist), that all the great phyla of the animal kingdom (including even the vertebrates) are now known to be found even in the Cambrian system, the earliest so-called "age" of the fossil column.

In summary, the creation model fits all the relevant known facts of science directly and would enable scientists to do a far better job of explaining and predicting scientific data than they ever could with the evolution model. It should be considered openly and seriously by all fair-minded people.

THE IMPACT OF ICR

The unique, California-based, organization known as the Institute for Creation Research has been described in many uncomplimentary terms by its numerous enemies in the educational and scientific establishments. Among the more colorful (and least objectionable) of these ascriptions have been "nerve center of the creation movement" and "creationist think tank."

Organized only in 1970 and reorganized in April 1972 under its present name, the Institute for Creation Research has been at the hub of the modern crationist revival which has been stirring nationwide and even worldwide interest in recent years. Featuring a variety of educational and research programs, the Institute (popularly known as ICR) has especially concentrated on its publications program, producing a broad spectrum of creation-oriented books and teaching materials, many of which have already had a great impact in both Christian and non-Christian circles.

The Institute's staff of scientist have published over 70 books since its inception, as well as hundreds of articles in various journals. Some of its books have been translated into about sixteen different languages. The monthly ICR periodical, *Acts & Facts*, which is sent on a complimentary basis to all who request it, has proved exceedingly popular and helpful.

Although all ICR publications[1] relate in some way to creationism or other areas of apologetics, the range of subjects and levels is quite broad. Included are a number of popular children's books, on the one hand, and a series of advanced technical monographs for scientific specialists on the other hand. A number of ICR books are designed specifically for public school use, containing no Biblical or religious material but showing that the scientific data all point to special creation rather than evolution. Some of the books are issued in both public school and general editions. A wide-ranging series of study modules is also available for actual classroom use in public schools. Many ICR books also have a strong Biblical emphasis. These include verse-by-verse commentaries on Genesis and Revelation, as well as textbooks on apologetics and popular expositions of Biblical creationism and Flood catastrophism.

The Institute for Creation Research has recently established the first evangelical and creationist graduate school of science in the Christian world, so far as known (by "evangelical" is meant commitment to full and sole Biblical inerrancy and authority in all fields of study). M.S. degree programs are now available in Astro-Geophysics, Biology, Geology and Science Education. In its fourth year of operation (1984-85), the enrollment had already included over sixty students, full and part-time, most of whom are well qualified and show great promise as future leaders.

---

1. A descriptive list of all ICR publications is available on request to the Institute for Creation Research, P.O. Box 2667 El Cajon, CA 92021, phone 619-440-2443.

Among ICR's best known activities have been the creation/evolution debates, over 180 of which have been held usually on leading campuses, sometimes drawing crowds of 5,000 or more. Creation seminars and lectures have been held by ICR scientists on many hundreds of campuses, as well as in hundreds of churches and other locations, in almost every state and Canadian province and in over 20 other nations around the world. A weekly radio program, "Science, Scripture and Salvation," is heard on over 90 U.S.A. stations, as well as overseas. Numerous Summer Institute and teachers' workshops have been held, as well as very many appearances on radio and television programs, both local and national. All of these activities are supported financially through the *Acts & Facts* mailing list, almost entirely by individual donations by concerned Christians.

Although there are now many other fine creationist organizations, both in this country and around the world,[1] ICR is unique in its staff of full-time scientists and support personnel, as well as in its broad complex of activities. Most observers have credited (or blamed) ICR as the chief influence in generating the modern revival of creationism.

A recent Associated Press poll has found that at least 86% of the American people now want creationist teachings to be brought back into the public schools. Since there are also now

---

1. Over 100 creationist organizations are listed in the writer's book, *History of Modern Creationism* (Master Books, 1984), pp. 341-347.

thousands of scientists who have become creationists, it is obvious that the creation movement is here to stay. Although a national consortium of establishment societies in science and education has been formed to combat creationism (with most of its attacks being leveled at ICR), interest in creation studies is bound to continue to increase. Even if the courts should ever decide to ban creationism from the public schools (a decision which would certainly be contrary to the intent of the original framers of the Constitution), this would only accelerate the already rapid proliferation of private Christian schools, almost all of which are strongly creationist in doctrine and philosophy.

Many people once thought that creationism, especially as taken seriously on a scientific level, had been destroyed at the Scopes trial in 1925. It may have gone underground for a time, as it were, but it is back today, alive and well! The main factor retarding a sweeping revival of creationism, in the national consciousness as well as in the schools and churches, is the continuing apathy of most evangelical Christians. We trust the Lord will soon begin to move in the minds and hearts of these also, for the need is great.

THE SPIRITUAL IMPACT OF CREATIONISM

In order to determine whether or not an emphasis on Biblical and scientific creationism was really effective in winning people to Christ and strengthening Christians in their faith and life, the Institute for Creation Research sent a detailed questionnaire to all people on its mailing list in 1976. Over 3,000 questionnaires were completed and returned. The results are listed and analyzed in the writer's book *King of Creation*

(Creation-Life Publishers, 1980, pp. 202-209), and
they clearly show that an informed and positive
emphasis on the fact and the implications of
special creation can be a tremendous tool for
soul-winning and spiritual growth. On the other
hand, Christians in general have been following a
compromising and yielding approach on this and
related issues for almost 200 years, with the net
result that a once-Christian society, sound in the
belief and practice of Biblical doctrine, has
become what many have called a "post-Christian"
society, humanistic in belief and pagan in practice.

In order to reconfirm and update the 1976
data, another questionnaire was sent early in
1984 to a random sample of the ICR *Acts & Facts*
readers, going to a total of 5,000 of the names on
our 75,000-name mailing list. Some 600 questionnaires were returned, an unusually good
response. The main purpose of this questionnaire
actually was to help the editors evaluate the
monthly "Impact" articles, and the returns indicated that these were very effective in meeting
the needs and interests of the readers.

However, the questionnaire also included one
question about ICR's spiritual impact. The question was: "In what ways have the ministries of
ICR (lectures, debates, books, radio broadcasts,
literature, etc.), been of *definite* spiritual help to
you?" The results, expressed as percentages
(some checked more than one category), were
as follows:

2% "Instrumental in leading me to Christ"
61% "Important to my spiritual growth as a
Christian"
22% "Effective in helping me win others to
Christ"

6%"Of little or no spiritual help"

37%"Other"

The comments made by many of those who checked "Other" indicates that they could easily have checked one or more of the first three categories. In any case, it is significant that at least 94% of those touched by the ICR creationist ministries considered them to be of definite spiritual impact for good in their lives. This survey strongly shows again that an uncompromising creationist emphasis in any Christian ministry would be abundantly fruitful, both in evangelism and Christian growth. It was also significant that the respondents indicated a high level of educational background. There were 8% who had doctoral degrees, 35% with masters' degrees, and 73% with bachelors' degrees. Only 1% had less than two years of college. The group as a whole certainly did not fit the stereotyped caricature of bigoted ignorant fundamentalists. The statistics were also reinforced by many fine personal testimonies, in the "Remarks" section of the questionnaire. Space allows only a small number of these to be included here, but they will help make the point. The following are typical:

> "I went through college, received B.S.Ed. in Biology, but was very vague about what I really believed. Your books have been my 'salvation' — my belief in the existence of God was beginning to waver."

> "Your materials were used of God to convert my life. When I first read *The Genesis Flood* and *Scientific Creationism*, my viewpoint turned around completely.

I accepted a position to teach science at
a Christian school in order to get this information out, and read nearly all of
your material. Using your Impact
articles, I taught creationism to our
students with an emphasis on
apologetics. Through creation seminars
that I was invited to present, God saw fit
to call me into the pastoral ministry.
Your materials are invaluable now to me
as a pastor to reproduce that work of
grace in members and friends of this
church. Keep it up!"

"*Scientific Creationism* was a major help
in resolving many conflicts between my
humanistic training in zoology and phar-
macology and my understanding of the
Scriptures and trust in my Lord."

"Helped me to find Christ as my own
personal Savior."

"It has given me good material for
witnessing (evidence, etc.) and also faith
building materials for my students."

"It has been good for my children's
growth in Christ. The study of creation
plus latest finds brings the Bible to life
and makes it relevant for today."

"I have found it effective in helping
others to grow spiritually too."

"Instrumental in showing me the scientific validity of creationism which changed
me from an evolutionist to a
creationist."

"I once was a 'Christian-evolutionist'(?)
but am now strictly a Biblical creationist."

> "Much of your material has helped me in leading home Bible studies."
>
> "Helps the training of my children."

These and many similar testimonies, along with the actual statistical data, make it evident that sound creationist ministries, both spoken and written, are not only effective scientifically, but are also being used by God to bring great spiritual blessing to those who are reached by them.

THE IMPORTANCE OF RECENT CREATION

Finally, there is one aspect of strict creationism which is under greater attack by evolutionists than any other. This is the Biblical doctrine of recent creation in six literal days. The evolutionist, encountering the weakness of the scientific case for evolution when he really tries to defend it, will almost always direct his own main arguments not against creation *per se*, but against recent creation and its corollary, flood geology.

As a result, some people who consider themselves creationists have been so intimidated against this Biblical concept that they try to cling to the nineteenth-century evolutionary compromise now known as the "day/age theory" and "progressive creation." Some still rely on the "gap theory," hoping they can ignore the problem by pigeon-holing the evolutionary ages of the geologists in an imaginary gap between the first two verses of Genesis. Both theories attempt to accommodate the geological ages, even though it is the geological ages which provide the main basis and framework for evolution. "Young-earth creationists" embarrass both the progressive creationists and the gap creationists, and so they

complain that recent creation is merely an
optional interpretation which is unimportant
and expendable.

But this cannot be. As a strictly scientific question, divorced from any Biblical or theological
considerations (as presumably, in a public school
textbook or in a scientific debate) the *date* of
creation can and perhaps should be treated as a
separate topic from the *fact* of creation. This does
not make it expendable, however. It is an important and basic issue that deserves serious study
in its own right, strictly in terms of the relevant
scientific data. When the Biblical and theological
data are also considered (as in a church or other
Christian context), the doctrine of recent creation
becomes critically significant, integrally inter-
woven with the doctrine of creation itself. Outlined
below, very briefly, are a few of the reasons why
the doctrine of recent creation is vitally important to true Biblical Christianity.

HISTORICAL REASONS

"Progressive creationism" is not a modern interpretation developed to bring the Genesis
record into harmony with modern science, but a
very ancient concept devised to impose a theistic
meaning upon the almost universal pagan
evolutionary philosophies of antiquity. The
eternal pre-existence of the physical universe of
space and time, with "matter" also present in
some form, was a belief shared by all ancient
religions and philosophies, seeking as they were
to function without an omnipotent, holy, eternal,
personal, Creator God. Sad to say, compromising
monotheists, both in ancient Israel and in the
early Christian church, repeatedly resorted to
various allegorical interpretations of Scripture,

involving some form of long-stretched-out
creation, seeking to combine
creationist/redemptionist theology with pagan
humanistic philosophy. Almost inevitably,
however, such compromises ended in complete
apostasy on the part of the compromisers.

In modern times, Charles Darwin himself is a
classic case in point. Starting out as a Biblical
creationist, his decline began with the acceptance of Lyellian uniformitarianism, the
geological ages and progressive creationism. He
then soon became a full-fledged theistic evolutionist and eventually an atheist. The same steps
were travelled by many other scientists of that
period. In fact, science itself was originally (in the
days of Newton and the other founders of modern
science) committed to the strict Biblical
chronology, then drifted into progressive creationism (after Cuvier, Lyell and others), then into
a Darwinian theistic evolutionism, finally into
total evolutionary naturalism.

The creationist revival of the first quarter of the
20th century was shortlived because it again
tried to compromise with the day-age theory. This
was Bryan's fatal mistake at the Scopes trial. The
various early creationist organizations also failed
to take a firm position on recent creationism and
soon either died out (e.g., The Religion and
Science Association, which lasted just two years,
and the Creation-Deluge Society, which survived
for six years), or became almost impotent (as in
the case of the Evolution Protest Movement) or
capitulated to theistic evolutionism (for example,
the American Scientific Affiliation). Multitudes of
churches, schools and other Christian organizations, have followed the same dead-end path of

compromise during the past century. For a fuller account, see *History of Modern Creationism* (by Henry M. Morris, Master Books, 1984, 384 pp.).

THEOLOGICAL REASONS

Even if one does not accept the Bible as the inerrant Word of God, the concept of a personal, omnipotent, omniscient, loving God is fatally flawed by the old-earth dogma. The very reason for postulating an ancient cosmos is to escape from God — to push Him as far away in space and as far back in time as possible, hoping thereby eventually to escape His control altogether, letting Nature become "god."

Surely an omniscient God could devise a better process of creation than the random, wasteful, inefficient trial-and-error charade of the so-called geological ages, and certainly a loving, merciful God would never be guilty of a creative process that would involve the suffering and death of multitudes of innocent animals, in the process of arriving at man millions of years later.

It should be obvious that the God of the Bible would create everything complete and good, right from the start. In fact, He testified that all of it was "very good" (Genesis 1:31). The wastefulness and randomness and cruelty which is now so evident in the world (both in the groaning creation of the present and in the fossilized world of the past) must represent an *intrusion* into His creation, not a mechanism for its accomplishment. God would never do a thing like that, except in judgment on sin!

Furthermore, if one must make a choice between a full-fledged theistic evolutionism and a compromising "progressive creationism," with its "day/age" theory of Genesis, one would have to judge the latter worse than the former, theologically speaking. Both systems are equally objectionable in terms of their common commitment to the geological age system, with its supposed three-billion-year spectacle of random wastefulness and a suffering, dying world. However, progressive creationism compounds the offense by making God have to redirect and recharge everything at intervals. Theistic evolutionism at least assumes a God able to plan and energize the total "creation" process right at the start. Progressive creationism imagines a world that has to be pumped up with new spurts of creative energy and guidance whenever the previous injection runs down or misdirects. Surely all those who *really* believe in the God of the Bible should see that *any* compromise with the geological-age system is theological chaos. Whether the compromise involves the day/age theory or the gap theory, the very concept of the geological ages implies divine confusion and cruelty, and the God of the Bible could never have been involved in such a thing as that at all.

BIBLICAL REASONS

As far as the Biblical record itself is concerned, there is not the slightest indication anywhere in Scripture that the earth endured long ages before the creation of Adam and Eve. The Lord Jesus Christ Himself said:

> "But from the beginning of the creation
> God made them male and female"
> (Mark 10:6).

The crystal-clear statement of the Lord in the Ten Commandments completely precludes the day/age interpretation of the six days of creation:

> "Remember the sabbath day, to keep it
> holy. Six days shalt thou labor, and do
> all thy work: But the seventh day is the
> sabbath of the Lord thy God: in it thou
> shalt not do any work, . . .: For in six
> days the Lord made heaven and earth,
> the sea, and all that in them is, and
> rested the seventh day: wherefore the
> Lord blessed the sabbath day, and
> hallowed it" (Exodus 20:8-11).

If God's six work days were not the same kind
of days as the six days of man's work week, then
God is not able to say what He means! The
language could hardly be more clear and explicit.
Note also its further confirmation later in the
book:

> "(The sabbath) is a sign between me and
> the children of Israel forever; for in six
> days the Lord made heaven and earth,
> and on the seventh day He rested, and
> was refreshed. And He gave unto Moses,
> when He had made an end of commun-
> ing with him upon Mount Sinai, two
> tables of testimony, tables of stone, writ-
> ten with the finger of God"
> (Exodus 31:17, 18).

All Scripture is divinely inspired, but this portion
was divinely *inscribed!*

Still further, the record of the six days of creation concludes with the statement by God that
everything in His creation was "very good" at the
end of the six days (Genesis 1:31). There is no
way this could be harmonized with a worldwide
fossil graveyard a mile deep all around the earth.
The Bible makes it plain, in fact, that death never
even entered the world until Adam sinned

(Romans 5:12; I Corinthians 15:21) and brought God's curse on the ground. (Genesis 3:17; Romans 8:20-22).

SCIENTIFIC REASONS

Those who insist on accommodating the geological ages, despite all the Biblical, theological and historical arguments against them, do so on the grounds that "science" requires it. "God would not deceive us," they say, "by making the earth look so old, if it were really young."

But it is really the other way around. If the earth were really old, God would not deceive us by saying so clearly and emphatically in His inspired Word that He created it all in six days.

For that matter, the earth does not really look old anyway. Evolutionists have tried to *make* it look old by imposing the unscriptural and unscientific dogma of uniformitarianism ("present processes are sufficient to explain all past geologic formations") on the geologic record of earth history as preserved in the rocks of the earth's crust. The fact is that geologists are today finally abandoning their outmoded nineteenth-century uniformitarianism, realizing that catastrophism ("past formations produced by intense convulsive processes") provides the only realistic explanation for the great geological structures of the earth. Even though they are still unwilling to acknowledge the validity of flood geology as based on the Bible, they do recognize now that the earth's various geological features were each formed rapidly, in intense catastrophes of one kind or another. Furthermore there are many times more geological processes[1] and systems (see *What is Creation Science?* by Henry M. Morris and Gary E. Parker (San Diego: Creation-Life Publishers, 1982), pp 239-259, for a listing of over 60 such processes) that imply a young age for the earth than the handful of radiometric methods that can be forced (through an extreme application of uniformitarianism) to yield an old age. This continued insistence on an ancient earth is purely because of the philosophical necessity to justify evolution and the pantheistic religion of eternal matter.

If it were not for the continued apathetic and compromising attitude of liberal and neo-evangelical Christian theologians and other intellectuals on this vital doctrine of recent creation, evolutionary humanism would long since have been exposed and defeated. The world will never take the Biblical doctrine of the divine control and imminent consummation of all things very seriously until we ourselves take the Biblical doctrine of the recent creation of all things seriously. Neither in space nor in time is our great God of creation and consummation "very far from every one of us" (Acts 17:27).

---

1.   See pp. 225-229.

Chapter II

The Strange God Of The Evolutionists

EVOLUTION AS RELIGION

Although evolutionists commonly claim that evolution is a fact of science, creationists have always maintained it is nothing but "science falsely so called" (I Timothy 6:20). It is a system which must be accepted on faith; all the real facts of science support creation rather than evolution, as will be discussed later.

Evolutionism is thus basically a religious philosophy. In fact, it is the fundamental world view underlying all religious and philosophical systems except those based on monotheism. If the universe was not created by an eternal, transcendent Creator, then the universe is the only ultimate reality. In that case, then all living creatures and other complex systems of the cosmos have supposedly evolved by natural processes from the space/matter/time universe itself. This concept is essentially what evolutionists believe.

Christians should certainly not be intimidated, however, by the incessant claims of evolutionists that this belief system is "science." The bombastic assertion that "*all* the facts of science support evolution" can usually be silenced by the challenge to cite just *one* scientific proof of real evolution! There is certainly no scientific evidence of "vertical" evolution occurring today, and there are no real transitional fossil structures to indicate that it ever took place in the past. No matter how old the universe may be, there is no scientific evidence that evolution could ever be possible and, even if it were possible, there is no real evidence that the universe is old enough for it to have happened. Evolution is religion, not science.

EVOLUTIONARY CREDULITY AMONG SCIENTISTS

In fact, it is not too much to say that one has to exercise a stronger faith to believe in evolution than in creation. This is often inadvertently admitted by evolutionists themselves.

Christian faith is essential for salvation (Ephesians 2:8) but in one sense it is not all that difficult to have this kind of faith. After all, the amazing majesty, beauty and complexity of the universe should make it easy to believe in a great Creator God (Psalm 19:1; Romans 1:20), and the overwhelming body of objective evidence for the historicity of the person and work of Jesus Christ — including His bodily resurrection from the grave — makes it easy enough to believe in His saving power.

But the faith of the evolutionist and humanist is of another order altogether. His is a splendid faith indeed, a faith not dependent on anything so mundane as evidence or logic, but rather a faith strong in childlike trust, relying wholly on omniscient Chance and omnipotent Matter to produce the complex systems and mighty energies of the universe.

The Harvard zoologist, P.D. Darlington, has penned a remarkable statement of this evolutionary faith, in his book *Evolution for Naturalists*. Acknowledging that the creative abilities of Matter are entirely enigmatic, he nevertheless bravely believes in them:

> "The outstanding evolutionary mystery now is how matter has originated and evolved, why it has taken its present form in the universe and on the earth, and why it is capable of forming itself into complex living sets of molecules. This capability is inherent in matter as we know it, in its organization and energy" (Wiley, 1980, p. 15).

Is not this a fine statement of faith? Even after looking down many avenues of potential evidence, Professor Darlington, more than 200 pages later, is still able to assert there is no evidence and thus his faith is still pure, blind faith.

> "It is fundamental evolutionary generalization that no external agent imposes life on matter. Matter takes the forms it does because it has the inherent capacity to do so. . . . This is one of the most remarkable and mysterious facts about our universe: that matter exists that has the capacity to form itself into the most complex patterns of life" (*Ibid.*, p. 233).

The evolutionist faces a great temptation here, a serious stumbling block to his faith. It seems utterly impossible that dead Matter could create Life. At this point, surely, he will have to defer to logic and acknowledge that Life must be produced by a Cause which is itself alive. After all, scientists long ago showed experimentally that life come only from life.

Ah, not so! His faith is strong enough to surmount even this barrier.

> "By this I do not mean to suggest the existence of a vital force or entelechy or universal intelligence, but just to state an attribute of matter as represented by the atoms and molecules we know. . . . We do not solve the mystery by using our inadequate brains to invent mystic explanations" (Ibid.).

This faith in the life-generating powers of Matter glows even more brightly in light of the confessed bafflement of those scientists most familiar with the nature of life and its supposed naturalistic[1] origin. One of these has said:

> We do not understand even the general features of the origin of the genetic code. . . . The origin of the genetic code is the most baffling aspect of the problem of the origins of life and a major conceptual or experimental breakthrough may be needed before we can make any substantial progress' (New Scientist, April 15, 1982, p. 151).

---

1 . There is really nothing "naturalistic" about these origin-of-life speculations. All of them involve assumed phenomena which are profoundly un-natural!

In fact, the author of this confession, Dr. Leslie Orgel, seems at first to have wavered somewhat in his own faith. He and Dr. Francis Crick, co-discoverer (with James Watson) of the remarkably complex DNA molecule, now known to be a basic component of life and of the genetic code which controls the reproduction of practically all living systems, have acknowledged that life was too complex to have arisen naturalistically in the few billion years of earth history.

In actuality, however, their credulous faith is still strong, perhaps even stronger than that of other evolutionists. They believe in "directed panspermia," the amazing notion that lifeseeds were somehow planted on earth by some unknown civilization from some other world in outer space! The very statement of this concept is itself a remarkable testimony to the grand credulity of the blind faith of these evolutionists, since there exists not one iota of scientific evidence for such celestial civilizations.

Another evolutionist of bold faith is Richard Dawkins, originator and popularizer of the strange concept of "selfish genes," an idea which itself bespeaks an unusual type of faith. Dawkins, who is on the faculty in zoology at England's famed Oxford University, maintains an unshakeable faith in Darwinian evolution, even at the molecular level, in spite of all the modern attacks thereon by fellow evolutionists. He acknowledges, of course, that the logical thing is to believe in God.

> "The more statistically improbable a thing is, the less can we believe that it just happened by blind chance. Super-

ficially the obvious alternative to chance is an intelligent Designer" (*New Scientist,* April 15, 1982, p. 130).

Even though it is, indeed, quite obvious that every complex and purposeful system which man has ever seen produced throughout history has been the product of an intelligent human designer, Professor Dawkins is willing to believe that life itself, far more complex than any man-made contrivance, was *not* designed. He dismisses God in these patronizing words:

> "I am afraid I shall give God rather short shrift. He may have many virtues: no doubt he is invaluable as a pricker of the conscience and a comfort to the dying and bereaved, but as an explanation of organized complexity he simply will not do. It is organized complexity we are trying to explain, so it is footling to invoke in explanation a being sufficiently organized and complex to create it" (*Ibid.*).

He is right, of course. It requires only a very ordinary sort of faith to explain a given effect by a cause adequate to produce the effect. Much more faith is required, an extra-ordinary faith, to believe that effects are produced by causes that are not able to produce them! To believe that non-living matter can create life, that chaotic disorder can evolve itself into organized complexity, that unthinking atoms can sort themselves into thinking human beings — *here is a noble faith!*

EVOLUTIONARY FAITH IN OTHER FIELDS

Evolutionary faith is not limited to biologists, of course. It can be appropriated by evolutionary humanists in philosophy, in economics, in politics, in all fields. A first-rate example was Adolph Hitler, whose implicit faith in Darwinism ("the preservation of favored races in the struggle for life," as the sub-title of Darwin's *Origin of Species* put it) gave him the vision and courage to array his assumed "master race" against the world, believing that its triumph would be for the greater good of all mankind in its ongoing evolutionary progress. Although his armies finally went down to defeat, he still retained his great faith!

> "Hitler believed in struggle as a Darwinian principle of human life that forced every people to try to dominate all others; without struggle they would rot and perish. . . . Even in his own defeat in April 1945, Hitler expressed his faith in the survival of the stronger and declared the Slavic peoples to have proven themselves the stronger" (P. Hoffman, *Hitler's Personal Security* [Pergamon, 1979], p. 264).

Note the strong and unselfish evolutionary faith of Adolph Hitler, willing even to sacrifice his entire Teutonic "race" and finally to take his own life, to advance the cause of evolution.

Finally, let us consider the remarkable faith of Isaac Asimov, the most prolific science writer of our generation. Asimov believes that our present universe began with the Big Bang of a primeval cosmic egg, whose initial explosion led to the formation of chemical elements, stars, galaxies and

finally people. Now note this fine statement
of faith.

> "The cosmic egg may be structureless
> (as far as we know), but it apparently
> represented a very orderly conglomera-
> tion of matter. Its explosion represented
> a vast shift in the direction of disorder,
> and ever since, the amount of disorder in
> the Universe has been increasing" (*In the
> Beginning,* Crown Pub., 1981, p. 24).

Now explosions commonly produce disorder
and disintegration, so this greatest of all explosions must have produced the ultimate in
disorder and disintegration. Evolution requires,
however, that the great Bang somehow yield
great order and complex structures. Dr. Asimov,
therefore, believes that the primeval egg possessed
an almost infinitely high degree of order, even
though it had no structure.

Herein we encounter Asimov's deep faith. In all
normal systems with which scientists work,
"structure" and "order" are essentially
synonymous, equivalent also to "information,"
"complexity," "organization," "integration" and
other such terms. If it did what evolutionists
believe it did, the primeval egg certainly must
have possessed a tremendous amount of organizing information and it thus seems nonsensical to
say it had no structure. Asimov believes not only
in run-of-the-mill impossibilities but in the
equivalence of opposites ("no structure" =
"high order").

However, Dr. Asimov does feel it necessary to
attempt some kind of rationalization, knowing
that people of lesser faith might otherwise
stumble.

> "The existence of the cosmic egg is, however, itself something of an anomaly. If the general movement of the universe is from order to disorder, how did the order (which presumably existed in the cosmic egg) originate? Where did it come from?" (*Ibid.*).

At this point, he makes another leap of faith, proposing that the universe — instead of expanding, as he believes it is doing now — was contracting, with everything somehow in reverse and with its order increasing as it contracted. For this to be possible, of course, gravitational attraction has to be invoked to pull it together. The problem with this belief, however, is that the known total mass of the matter in the universe is a hundred times too small to allow this ever to happen.

Such a problem as this does not overcome the faith of an Asimov. He can handle it merely by another act of faith.

> "I have a hunch that the 'missing mass' required to raise the density to the proper figure will yet be found and that the universe will yet be discovered to oscillate" (*Ibid.*, p. 25).

Asimov's hunch, therefore, solves it all.

We creationists, admittedly, find it difficult to believe all these things that evolutionists manage to believe. But we have always had a high regard for the principle of faith, even though our own faith is rather ordinary, based as it is on such strong evidence as almost to compel belief in the God of creation and redemption. We must, therefore, at least express admiration for the remarkable faith of the evolutionist.

EVOLUTION IN OTHER RELIGIONS

Christians need to be aware of the important fact that there are really *only two basic religions* in the world. One is God-centered, the other is man-centered. Thus, the basic choice is limited either to monotheistic ("one God") creationism or evolutionary pantheistic ("all-god") humanism. Biblical Christianity is founded on the truth that there is only one God and that He is both the Creator and Redeemer of the world. Although orthodox Judaism and Islam are also monotheistic religions, they fail to recognize that the God who created all things is the only one who can be the true Savior of all things, through His incarnation and sacrificial death as Son of God and Son of Man. Both Jews and Moslems, therefore, persist in believing in salvation by human works, rather than by faith in the only possible effective work of redemption, the death and resurrection of the only true Creator God, the Lord Jesus Christ. Thus, in the ultimate sense, they also become religious humanists, relying on the ability of men and women to save themselves. In the last analysis, only a fully-Biblical Christianity can be a true monotheistic, creationist faith, centered altogether in the Person and work of the one true God, Creator and Savior, through Jesus Christ.

As far as all the other great world religions are concerned — Buddhism, Confucianism, Taoism, Hinduism, Sikhism, Shintoism, Animism, and others — all of these are frankly pantheistic (or polytheistic, which amounts to the same thing). None of them believe in a transcendent Creator of the entire universe of space and time. To them, the cosmos itself is the ultimate reality, eternally existing, and capable of generating by its own powers all the complex systems in nature, including animals and human beings and even unseen spirits. The latter may be understood either as the spirits of dead ancestors and/or as the "gods" — angels, demons, or other spirit beings who influence the physical world and the affairs of human life. To the more sophisticated philosophers of these religions, these gods and goddesses may be viewed as personifications of the various forces and systems of nature, the different faces, as it were, of the one great Intelligence or Force which pervades the cosmos, Nature itself (with a capital "N"). This, of course, is pantheism ("all-god"), but it could as well be called atheism ("no god"). If "god" is everywhere in general, then such a god could never really be distinctively anywhere in particular.

All of the above analysis would apply equally well to the religions of antiquity, such as those of the Greeks and Romans, Egyptians and Babylonians, and all the rest. None believed (or believe) in a personal omnipotent Creator who called the entire cosmos (space, time, energy, matter, life, spirit) into being by His own eternal power.

Therefore, to all intents and purposes, all of these religions — ancient and modern — are fundamentally evolutionary religions. They are based ultimately on faith in the "creature," rather than the Creator (Romans 1:25), and therefore they are all really the *same* religion. It is not surprising, therefore, that they have all adapted easily to modern "scientific" evolutionism, since the latter is merely a slightly modernized form of their ancient nature/spirit worship anyhow. Consequently, evolution is now taught just as thoroughly and easily in the school systems of

Asia and Africa and the islands of the sea as it is in the schools of Europe and America.

As a typical example, consider the religion of China, both ancient and modern. A recent book, *China and Charles Darwin,* by James R. Pusey (Harvard University Press, 1983, 544 pp.) shows clearly that the evolutionistic nature of China's ancient religions (Confucianism, Taoism, Buddhism, Animism) contributed directly to the easy assimilation of Chinese culture by the modern evolutionist religion of Marxism. Darwinist philosopher Michael Ruse, reviewing the book, makes the following analysis:

> "(Darwin's) ideas took root at once, for China did not have the innate intellectual and religious barriers to evolution that often existed in the West. Indeed, in some respects, Darwin seemed almost Chinese! . . . Taoist and neo-Confucian thought had always stressed the 'thingness' of humans. Our being at one with the animals was no great shock." ("The Long March of Darwin," *New Scientist,* Vol. 103, August 16, 1984, p. 35).

The transition from western Darwinism to Marxism and communism was then easy, once the influence of Christian missions in China had been undermined.

> "As with American industrialists, what made Darwinism attractive were the notions of struggle, and survival, and (most particularly) success. . . . Today, the official philosophy is Marxist-Leninism (of a kind). But without the secular, materialist approach of Darwinism

> (meaning now the broad social
> philosophy), the ground would not have
> been tilled for Mao and his revolu-
> tionaries to sow their seed and reap their
> crop." (*Ibid.*)

It is preposterously hypocritical, therefore, for
the opponents of creationism to insist that, since
the latter is "religious," it should not be taught in
the schools. Evolution is much more of a religion
than is creation, requires more credulous faith
than does creation, and is the basis of many
more formal religious systems than is creation.
The evolutionary humanists don't want *religion*,
as such, banned from the schools. They only want
true religion banned!

EVOLUTION AS UN-REALISM

One might suppose that such a universal
religious system as evolution must be based on
good evidence, but it is not so! A surprising admission appears in a recent issue of *Nature*, the
prestigious British science magazine. Evolution is
there finally acknowledged to be contrary to all
observation and common sense.

> "Most contemporary scientists have dif-
> ficulty understanding the appeal of alleg-
> ed scientific arguments of creation
> science to popular common sense. Evolu-
> tion may have scientific experts on its
> side, but it strains popular common
> sense. It is simply difficult to believe
> that the amazing order of life on Earth
> arose spontaneously out of the original
> disorder of the universe" (George M.
> Marsden, "Creation vs. Evolution: No

Middle Way" *Nature*, V. 305, October 13, 1983, p. 572).

Dr. Marsden was one of the evolutionist witnesses at the infamous Arkansas creation-law trial. He makes the fascinating comment that "there are an unusual number of engineers in the creation science movement" and that creation science "is close to that which works best for engineers, straightforward, consistent, factual, with no nonsense." (*Ibid.*).

As an engineer myself, I have long contended the same thing. Engineering science is based on confirmed principles of science, together with empirical testing. Complex systems in engineering required careful and intelligent design. To believe that the far more complex systems of living organisms could ever arise by chance is indeed contrary to common sense, as well as all experience.

Marsden calls creation science "naive realism" which is not at all "anti-scientific in principle" (p. 573). This seems to be an unintended confession that evolution "science" is essentially "sophisticated unrealism." People believe in evolution in spite of the fact that it is based on no empirical evidence, there are no records of it in the past, it contradicts the basic laws of science, and is an insult to common sense! Marsden, although *believing* in it strongly enough to support it in court, calls it "the key mythological element in a philosophy that functions as a virtual religion" (p. 574).

One would be hard put to find a more appropriate commentary on evolutionary reasoning than II Corinthians 4:3, 4:

"But if our gospel be hid, it is hid to them that are lost: In whom the god of this world hath blinded the minds of them that believe not, lest the light of the glorious gospel of Christ, who is the image of God, should shine unto them."

THE GOD OF THE HUMANISTS

There are, of course, different "cults" among the evolutionary humanists, just as there are various "denominations" among Bible-believing Christians. Some are outspoken materialistic atheists, such as those in Madalyn Murray O'Hair's American Atheist Association, centered in Austin, Texas. They profess to believe in no god of any sort and are opposed, they say, to any form of religion — occultism and eastern mysticism as well as Biblical fundamentalism and everything else. To them, "science" itself comes closest to being the equivalent of God.

Many others, particularly among intellectuals, seem to practice a more genteel form of atheism, professing certain seemingly noble and humanitarian ideals. They prefer to be known as "secular humanists" or even "religious humanists." The latter tend to overlap with those in many types of pantheistic religious associations, some of which even call themselves churches. All kinds of eastern mystics, occultic movements, philosophical clubs, socialistic communes, lodges, and miscellaneous other organizations believe and practice what, to all intents and purposes, is the religion of humanism. The pantheistic god whom they worship may be called "the Force," "Nature," "the World Soul," "the Intelligent Universe," "Love," or any one of many other names, but it is never the God of the Bible, the eternal Creator. Many of the people and organizations involved in these variant forms of evolutionary humanism seem to be interlocked in many devious ways in a vast complex network which some call the "New Age Movement" or "The Aquarian Conspiracy" (see *The Hidden Dangers of the Rainbow,* by Constance Cunby, published by Huntington House, 1983, 268 pp.).

These are dangerous paths to follow, and too many Christians already have been tempted to compromise with the teachings and practices of such systems and organizations. "Thou shalt have no other gods before me!" thundered the God of creation, in the very first of His ten commandments (Exodus 20:3). "There shall no strange god be in thee; neither shalt thou worship any strange god" (Psalm 81:9).

Men through the centuries have stubbornly gone after many strange (or "alien") gods, and have perversely "worshipped and served the creature more than the Creator, who is blessed for ever. Amen" (Romans 1:25). Yet none have ever been stranger or more opposed to the true God of heaven than the god of the evolutionary humanists of these last days.

One leading spokesman of modern humanism is Rev. Lester Mondale, brother of former vice-president Walter Mondale. In a remarkable article entitled "False Gods," Mondale first repudiated the God of the Bible:

> "Humanistically committed, . . .
> Although I sympathize with Elijah's repugnance of false gods, I must observe . . . that Elijah's Yahweh is also false. . . . What holds for the typical godhead Father holds also for the Son." (*The*

Humanist, Vol. 44, January/February 1984, p. 33).

Then, he proceeded to describe what he would consider to be the character and attributes of the humanist's god, and these are, indeed, alien to those of the true God of creation. Then, looking for such a god, he wrote:

> "There is always the philosophical possibility that someone, somewhere, might come up with God, the real thing. . . . In any case, I feel certain that, in holding fast to the standards, values and culture by which we are driven to judge false gods as false, we are vastly closer to the moral character a real Supreme Being would be likely to exemplify were He(?) to over come the world with an authentic First Coming" (*Ibid.*, p. 34).

More frankly atheistic even than Rev. Mondale is one of the most vitriolic anticreationist humanists of our day, Dr. Isaac Asimov, famous science fiction author and the most prolific of all science writers. In a 1982 fund-raising letter sent out on behalf of the American Civil Liberties Union and its anticreationist activities, Asimov wrote:

> "These religious zealots . . . are marching like an army of the night into our public schools with their Bibles held high. . . . And they pose a very real threat in a society that esteems academic freedom and enlightenment over dogma and moral righteousness."

Asimov's concern is that of a committed atheistic humanist, fearful that evolutionism may be losing its longtime control over America's public schools. In his commentary on Genesis (an unusual project for an atheist!) he wrote:

> "Science describes a Universe in which it is not necessary to postulate the existence of God at all" (*In the Beginning*, 1981, p. 13).

He may think it unnecessary to believe in *God*, but Asimov does have a remarkable faith in *naturalism*. He believes that the marvelously complex universe has evolved from the supposed primeval Big Bang. That is, even highly organized living systems have somehow developed naturalistically from the profound disorder of a cosmic explosion (see the discussions of Asimov's faith on pp. 53-55).

Rev. Mondale, Dr. Asimov and their humanistic colleagues are still looking for the "first coming" of their god into the world, but when "He(?)" does come, this god "opposeth and exalteth himself above all that is called God, . . . showing himself that he is God" (II Thessalonians 2:4). The god of humanism will be a great representative Man, "and he shall exalt himself above every god, and shall speak marvelous things against the God of gods, . . . Neither shall he regard . . . any god: for he shall magnify himself above all" (Daniel 11:36-37). Humanism, based as it is on the false cosmogony of evolution, will inevitably culminate in the worship of the ultimate false "man" as the ultimate strange "god."

THE TRAGIC HERITAGE OF MODERN SCIENTIFIC EVOLUTIONISM

The legacy of Charles Darwin has not been an enlightened age of scientific progress, as his afficionados proclaim. Instead the triumph of Darwinism was followed by over a century of the worst barbarism and cruelty (always "justified" by its practitioners in the name of evolutionary "science") that the world has ever experienced. North America, because of its Biblical Christian heritage, has not yet been thrown into this maelstrom of anti-God bitterness, but many other parts of the world have experienced it, and our time may be coming.

This is a very sensitive, even explosive, subject, and western evolutionists usually react angrily and sarcastically when it is mentioned. This in turn intimidates many Christians — even creationists — who, therefore, also tend to react negatively against those who bring it up.

Nevertheless, it is a very true and very important fact that evolutionary philosophical rationalizations have been used to justify all sorts of evil social and economic systems and all kinds of deplorable personal behavior and practices in this post-Darwin era. People do need to know this, especially Christian people. As Christ reminded us long ago; "A corrupt tree bringeth forth evil fruits" (Matthew 7:17). Likewise, the apostle James reminded us that "no fountain can yield both salt water and fresh" (James 3:12). The fountain itself must be cleansed, and the corrupt tree cut down, if the householder wants to stop the flow of bitter water and the production of deadly fruit. It is dangerous to eat and drink mixtures of the good and bad, for the bad can only contaminate the good.

It is obvious, of course, that the evils implicit in the evolutionary system do not mean that every individual evolutionist necessarily manifests the same evils in his own thinking or practice. But

the dangers *are there* in the very nature of the
system, and history confirms the tragic results in
far too many lives.

THE TENETS OF HUMANISM

The well-known Humanist Manifesto of 1933,
largely formulated under the guidance of
educator/philosopher John Dewey, has only in recent years received the attention from Christians
that it warrants. Since they have had profound
impact on American schools and society for half
a century now, the fifteen Tenets of Humanism,
as set forth in this Manifesto, surely need to be
read, and their significance comprehended by
every concerned Christian and every concerned
American. Originally published in the May/June
issue of *The New Humanist* (Vol. 6, 1933), they
have been republished in many places since, and
are easily available, either from the American
Humanist Association itself (Amherst, NY) or as
reproduced in many other publications, both
Christian and non-Christian (an excellent Christian exposition is contained in the Bill Gothard
study book *How to Understand Humanism*,
published in 1984 by the Institute in Basic Youth
Conflicts, Oak Brook, Illinois).

Tenet No. 1 states: "Religious humanists regard
the universe as self-existing and not created."
Tenet No. 2 continues: "Humanism believes that
man is a part of nature and that he has emerged
as the result of a continuous process." Thus, the
evolution of the universe and of man, both
without benefit of God's action, are acknowledged
as the very foundation of humanism. All the other
tenets (including one advocating a global communistic form of government) are based on the
first two. All the multitudinous other beliefs and

practices of the secular humanists stem from
their implicit faith that there is no transcendent
Creator God to whom they are responsible. The
second Humanist Manifesto, issued in 1973 (*The
Humanist,* October 1973) reaffirmed and
amplified these Tenets. Among other things, the
new Manifesto proclaimed: "As non-theists, we
begin with humans, not God — nature, not deity.
. . . No deity will save us; we must save
ourselves."

If there is no God, then all the systems of the
cosmos must have evolved either by mechanistic
chance or by some mystical power resident in the
structure and processes of the cosmos itself. In
either case, *Homo sapiens* is the highest achieve-
ment of the evolutionary process, and so man
and/or woman become, to all intents and purposes, "gods." This is humanism.

Since this is the case, the measure of right and
wrong ceases to be the absolute moral law
enacted by the Creator (not even what some have
called "natural law"), but only what most benefits
mankind and the ongoing process of evolution.
The decision as to what this may be in a particular case is to be made by the "State," which
presumably represents corporate mankind. In
practice, this may well become the "Head of
State" — some great superman who manages to
acquire the power to dictate to his fellow humans
what they must do or not do, all in the name of
"society," or "the people," or "the greatest good
for the greatest number," or some other such
noble-sounding but self-serving slogan.

Thus, the great assortment of modern social
practices which Biblical fundamentalists (and
political conservatives also) are fighting today —
including abortion, homosexuality, pornography,

euthanasia, divorce, promiscuity, use of drugs, and other such anti-Christian activities — are essentially nothing but logical outworkings of the evolutionary philosophy. This does not mean, of course, that every woman who submits to an abortion or every teenager who tries hallucinogenic drugs is an evolutionary humanist. People commit sins for all kinds of personal and ephemeral reasons and this is unfortunately true for Christians as well as atheists. What it does mean is that the intellectual rationale for such practices, whenever their defenders try to analyze and justify them scientifically, is basically a rejection of the Biblical world view in favor of the evolutionary world view.

ABORTIONISM AND THE RECAPITULATION THEORY

Consider, for example, the terrible holocaust of abortionism that has been unleashed on our nation in recent years as a result of decisions by a humanist-dominated court system. What once was considered a serious crime is now considered a "human right" — that is, the so-called right of the mother to control her own body. Little, if any, consideration is given to the rights of the unborn child, for the simple reason that the fetus is now regarded as "not fully human." The basis of this inhuman decision is simply the evolutionary view of man.

> "So the abortion debate has its roots in two alternative ways of imagining the unborn. Our civilization, until recently, agreed in imagining the unborn child on the pattern of the incarnation, which maximizes his dignity; but many people

now imagine him on the pattern of evolution, as popularly understood, which minimizes his dignity." (Joseph Sobran, "The Averted Gaze," *Human Life Review,* Spring 1984, p. 6. Sobran is a nationally syndicated columnist.)

This "pattern of evolution" as popularly understood is nothing else than the hoary evolutionary belief that "ontogeny recapitulates phylogeny." As Sobran says:

"The adage has been discredited, of course, but this does not mean it has lost its power over the imagination of many modern people. They still suppose that the human fetus is in the early stages of development a 'lower' form of life, and this is probably what they mean when they say it isn't 'fully human.' It begins as something virtually amoebic, proceeds to become something like a shrimp, then a puppy, then an ape, and finally a human" (*Ibid.*).

If the embryo is merely recapitulating the animal stages of its evolutionary ancestry, then it is all right to terminate it before it becomes human, so the reasoning goes. The fact is, however, that this bizarre notion has long since been disproved. As leading evolutionist S.J. Gould admits, commenting on the recapitulation theory:

"In Down's day, the theory of recapitulation embodied a biologist's best guide for the organization of life into sequences of higher and lower forms. (Both the theory and 'ladder approach' to classification that it encouraged are, or should be, defunct today)." ("Dr. Down's Syndrome," *Natural History,* Vol. 89, April 1980, p. 144.)

ONTOGENY, PHYLOGENY AND EVOLUTION IN PRACTICE

This most bizarre of the supposed evidences for organic evolution was popularized in the nineteenth century by the atheistic biologist Ernst Haeckel, who also headed Germany's infamous Monist League and soon "became one of Germany's major ideologists for racism, nationalism, and imperialism." (Daniel Gasman, *The Scientific Origins of National Socialism: Social Darwinism in Ernst Haeckel and the German Monist League,* published by American Elsevier, 1971, p. xvii.) Also known as the so-called "biogenetic law," or the recapitulation theory, it has always been known in terms of the textbook slogan "ontogeny recapitulates phylogeny," meaning "the embryonic development of each growing embryo in the womb repeats the evolutionary development of its species." The human embryo, for example, was said to begin life as a protozoan, then go through a fish stage (with gill slits) and a monkey stage (with a tail) before finally becoming a human being.

This absurd theory has long since been repudiated by competent biologists, even though it still crops up in some textbooks and anticreationist polemics. Any lingering hope that it might be true should have been demolished by modern fetoscopy, which "makes it possible to observe directly the unborn child through a tiny telescope inserted through the uterine wall" (*Parents,* October 1979, p. 50). Dr. Sabine Schwabenthan says:

"We now know, for instance, that man, in his prenatal stages, does not go through the complete evolution of life — from a primitive single cell to a fishlike water creature to man. Today it is known that every step in the fetal development process is specifically human" (*Ibid.*)

For a false notion, however, the recapitulation theory has had profound and tragic consequences. During the early days of paleontology, "progressive creationist" geologists such as Agassiz and D'Orbigny, following Cuvier, frequently used it as a framework for arranging their fossils in what they assumed should be a chronological sequence, on their pure assumption that God's successive creations should conform to their arrangement for classifying animals and also to the embryological development of each animal. The paleontological series so constructed naturally later seemed to give a superficial appearance of evolution, even though it included no real "transitional" forms, and even though it had little relation to any vertical successions of sedimentary strata. It was by this questionable device that the "fossil record" so constructed later began to be cited as the main proof of evolution.

Also, as Harvard's Stephen Jay Gould has pointed out:

"Recapitulation provided a convenient focus for the pervasive racism of white scientists; they looked to the activities of their own children for comparison with normal, adult behavior in lower races" (*Natural History*, April 1980, p. 144).

According to Gould, the term "mongoloid" was first applied to mentally defective people because it was then commonly believed that the Mongoloid race had not yet evolved to the status of the Caucasian race. Similarly, Henry Fairfield Osborn, the leading American paleontologist of the first half of the twentieth century, argued that:

> "The Negroid stock is even more ancient than the Caucasian and Mongolian, . . . The standard of intelligence of the average adult Negro is similar to that of the eleven-year-old youth of the species *Homo sapiens*" (*Natural History*, April 1980, p. 129).

As noted above, Haeckel (and his disciple Adolph Hitler) used it to justify the myth of the Aryan super-race, destined to subjugate or obliterate other races.

But all these tragic results of this false theory are dwarfed by the painful murders of millions of unborn children. Since 1973, over 15 million babies have been murdered by abortion, more than twice the number of Jews slain by the Nazis under Hitler. The only possible "scientific" rationalization for these atrocities is the standard argument that the unborn fetus is not yet really a human being at all, a widespread belief that can only be based on the evolutionary philosophy in general and this same old discredited recapitulation theory in particular. After all, it is not considered murder to kill mere animals.

Ideas do have consequences, and false ideas can have tragic and lethal consequences. The slogan "ontogeny recapitulates phylogeny" is not only a curious but discredited slogan of the past.

It is also the root of a tree bearing deadly fruit in the present.

EVOLUTION AND ANIMALISTIC BEHAVIOR

Evolutionary reasoning is also behind the current widespread attempts to legitimize the practice of homosexuality. This ancient sin has only recently been alleged to be acceptable behavior, and the argument has been that Biblical condemnations should no longer be considered, since such actions are claimed to be based on genetic inheritance and are therefore "natural," as in other animals.

Similar arguments are offered for the so-called sexual revolution. Since men and women are merely higher animals, so they say, it is supposedly natural for their sexual behavior to be animalistic. Biblical moral standards are no longer definitive or authoritative, of course, since evolutionary "science" has supposedly disproved the Bible.

Following their prophet, the atheist Aldous Huxley (brother of Julian), who was probably the first leading intellectual to urge them to do so, followed later by Timothy Leary and others, people began to use hallucinogenic drugs in search of religious insights and experiences which they had lost when the true God was taken away from them by the "scientific" evolutionary humanism of their teachers. Thus was born our modern "drug culture."

Another type of evil in society, the use of violence to obtain what one desires, has also been justified by evolutionary reasoning. Ever since Raymond Dart discovered the first fossil of *Australopithecus* in the mid-1920s, along with what he thought were "tools" used by these so-called "hominids," (or ape-like ancestors of man), it has been widely held that these creatures were carnivorous "killer apes," who slaughtered animals and probably other hominids for food and possibly for conquest or even sport. This attribute of these presumed humanoid ancestors of man supposedly "explains" and even "justifies" man's instinctive drive to conquer and loot and kill. This "cave-man" caricature of ancient men and women has been inordinately popularized in comic strips and motion pictures and even school books for many years, but anthropologists now know it is false. The bones of animals supposedly slaughtered, skinned, scraped and eaten by the australopithecines had been misinterpreted all along.

> "They concluded that the australopithecines, like the baboons and antelopes from the same deposits, had been dragged into the caves and eaten by leopards and carnivores. Most and probably all of the bone tools were scraps from a cat's lunch — and so were the remains of the supposed killer apes" (Matt Cartmill, *Natural History*, Vol. 92, November 1983, p. 76).

Men and women may be prone to all sorts of violent and selfish behavior, but this is because of sin in their hearts, not animals in their ancestry. It needs to be condemned and judged, unless first repented, forgiven and forsaken — not coddled and justified on the basis of evolutionary presuppositions, as courts have been so quick to do in recent decades.

Still another animalistic practice is now beginning to be advocated, on the basis of evolutionism.

Once abortionism has become acceptable, infanticide cannot be far behind, as well as other checks on population growth (euthanasia, etc.).

> "Among some animal species, then, infant killing appears to be a natural practice. Could it be natural for humans too, a trait inherited from our primate ancestors? . . . Charles Darwin noted in *The Descent of Man* that infanticide has been 'probably the most important of all checks' on population growth throughout most of human history" (Barbara Burke, "Infanticide," *Science 84*, May 1984).

There have already been many attempts even at genocide in the name of evolutionary progress, such as the slaughter of the aborigines in Tasmania by white settlers, who argued that these "primitives" were not really human; the gas ovens of Nazi Germany, in the name of Aryan racial supremacy; and others.

If evolution is the real law of life, then practices such as these may really contribute to the overall progress of evolution, as their practitioners allege. It is hard to offer an effective scientific argument against them, if evolution is true.

THE EVOLUTIONARY BASIS OF DEADLY SOCIAL PHILOSOPHIES

Many writers, both Christian and non-Christian, have also pointed out the evolutionistic base of such deadly social philosophies as communism and Nazism, as well as racism and laissez-faire capitalism. Modern evolutionists react angrily when attention is called to this fact, but it *is* a fact, as can be easily confirmed in the literature of the theoreticians and practitioners of each of these systems.

In the last half of the nineteenth century, a widespread philosophy known as social Darwinism dominated the thinking of many of the industrial tycoons of the era.

> "As the steel magnate Andrew Carnegie put it after reading Darwin and Spencer: 'Not only had I got rid of theology and the supernatural, but I had found the truth of evolution. *All is well since all grows better* became my motto, my true source of comfort.' " (cited in Edward Kirkland's "Introduction" to Carnegie's essay *The Gospel of Wealth,* published by Harvard University Press, 1962).

Similar philosophies were expressed by such men as John D. Rockefeller, the oil baron, James Hill, the railroad magnate, and numerous others, all impressed by the teachings of Herbert Spencer in England and William Grant Sumner in the United States, centered in the famous slogan "struggle for existence and survival of the fittest."

This right-wing type of Darwinism also led to racism and imperialism, and even to fascism and Hitlerism, whereas a left-wing approach to evolutionary thought became basic in Marxist-Leninism and communism. Both systems are anti-creationist, anti-Biblical and anti-Christian, and even when they fight with each other, they remain united in opposition to creationism and Biblical fundamentalism.

The Christian philosopher Francis Schaeffer has commented incisively on the Darwinian basis of German militarism and Nazism:

"Later, these ideas helped produce an
even more far-reaching yet logical conclusion: the Nazi movement in Germany.
Heinrich Himmler (1900-1945), leader of
the Gestapo, stated that the law of
nature must take its course in the survival of the fittest. The result was the
gas chambers. Hitler stated numerous
times that Christianity and its notion of
charity should be 'replaced by the ethic
of strength over weakness. . . . Thus,
many factors created the situation. But
in that setting the theory of the survival
of the fittest sanctioned what occured"
(*How Should We Then Live?*, Revell, 1976,
p. 151).

THE EVOLUTIONARY FICTION OF RACE

Another "right-wing" aspect of evolutionary
humanism is the belief system known as racism,
promoted especially in Nazi Germany and defended
there and elsewhere on the basis of Haeckel's
famous but long-disproved recapitulation theory,
as already discussed. White racism was also advocated by Charles Darwin, Thomas Huxley, and
most other leading evolutionists of the nineteenth and early twentieth centuries.

James Ferguson has recently reminded us that
the quasi-scientific evolutionary racism of the
nineteenth century had a deadly impact on
the world.

"In nineteenth-century Europe the concept of race was a preoccupation for the
growing human sciences. . . . These first
physical anthropologists helped to
develop the concept of Aryan supremacy,

> which later fueled the institutional
> racism of Germany in the 1930's, and of
> South Africa today." ("The Laboratory of
> Racism," *New Scientist*, Vol. 103,
> September 27, 1984, p. 18).

Similarly, Stephen Jay Gould has noted that
evolutionary anthropologists were long convinced
that the various "races" all had separate evolutionary origins and thus had "evolved" to different levels of intelligence and ability during
their long histories.

> "We cannot understand much of the
> history of late nineteenth and early
> twentieth-century anthropology, with its
> plethora of taxonomic names proposed
> for nearly every scrap of fossil bone,
> unless we appreciate its obession with
> the identification and ranking of races."
> ("Human Equality is a Contingent Fact of
> History," *Natural History*, Vol. 93,
> November 1984, p. 28).

And, since these anthropologists all were white
Europeans or Americans, they were confident that
the Caucasian race had advanced far above the
"lower" races. Gould himself rejects racism,
however, on the shaky grounds that human
separation into racial subdivisions is too "recent"
for significant differences to have developed.

> ". . . the division of humans into modern
> 'racial' groups is a product of our recent
> history. It does not predate the origin of
> our own species, *Homo sapiens*, and pro-
> bably occurred during the last few tens
> (or at most hundreds) of thousands of
> years." (*Ibid.*, p. 31.)

Dr. Gould, however, seems to be arguing against himself here. If the "races" have been segregated for possibly a "few hundreds of thousands of years," then it is completely arbitrary to assume that no significant racial differences would evolve in such immense spans of time — that is, if evolution were really true. Gould's own concept of punctuated equilibrium involves evolutionary "jerks" which produce significant evolutionary changes in only a few generations. Evolutionism — whether the slow and gradual changes of neo-Darwinism or the rapid jumps of punctuationism — is, by its very nature, racist in its implications.

In contrast, Biblical creationism, with its record of the *recent* origin of all the tribes and nations after the great Flood, only a few thousand years ago, makes real "races," in the evolutionary sense, quite impossible. This fact, of course, correlates perfectly with the Biblical teaching that there is only one race — the human race!

As a matter of fact, the very idea of "race" is strictly an evolutionary concept, though it did not originate with Darwin. Darwin appropriated it from previous evolutionists, and even gave his famous book (*Origin of Species*) the subtitle "The Preservation of Favored Races in the Struggle for Life." As far as the Bible is concerned, neither the word nor the concept of race appears anywhere in Scripture. The Bible teaches clearly that all people are of "one blood," descended from Noah and his three sons in only a few thousand years, not nearly enough to develop real races in the evolutionary sense (that is, sub-species in the process of evolving into new species).

This also is a fact not known or appreciated by most Christians. All the tensions and tragedies of

racial conflicts stem from racist philosophy,
which is squarely based on an evolutionary view
of human origins and history. R.W. Wrangham,
reviewing this subject, has said:

> "Even if particular individuals from dif-
> ferent populations occasionally look
> alike, surely the distinctions between
> whole populations are big enough to
> justify calling them racial. This was the
> dominant view from the mid-18th cen-
> tury onward. . . . Authors varied in their
> opinion of the number of human races,
> from Cuvier's three to as many as thirty
> or more in the 20th century, but with few
> exceptions they agreed that the concept
> of race was sound" (*American Scientist*,
> Vol. 72, January/February 1984, p. 75).

Similarly, anthropologist Russell Tuttle, of the
Univesity of Chicago, in reviewing an article by
Loring Brace, says:

> Brace squarely confronts racist in-
> fluences in the two chief founders of in-
> stitutional physical anthropology in the
> United States . . . [Ales] Hrdlicka, based
> at the American Museum of Natural
> History, and E.A. Hooton, with whom
> most of the second generation of
> physical anthroplogists studied at
> Harvard" (*Science*, Vol. 220,
> 1982, p. 832).

Dr. Brace (with whom I once had a
creation/evolution debate) is, like Tuttle, a
leading modern evolutionary anthropologist, at
the University of Michigan. Hrdlicka and Hooton,
along with Henry Fairfield Osborn, also at the

American Museum of Natural History, were leading American anthropologists of the first half of the twentieth century, and all were scientific racists, as Tuttle says. In fact, Osborn even taught that the Negro "race" was actually a lower species than *Homo sapiens!* (*Natural History,* April 1980, p. 129). For an extended account of the "scientific" racism held by most nineteenth century evolutionary scientists, see *Outcasts from Evolution,* by John S. Haller, Jr. (University of Illinois Press, 1971, 228 pp.).

However, the current generation of anthropologists, largely because of anti-racist pressures from the liberal and Marxist "left-wing" of evolutionary thought, are finally beginning to abandon the ideas of race altogether, and thus are inadvertently returning to the Biblical concept. Tuttle says:

> "(Brace) reiterates the modern view that we should abandon the concept of race altogether and instead record the gene frequencies and traits of populations that are identified simply by their geographic localities. This genotypic and phenotypic information is to be interpreted in terms of historical and proximate selective forces" (Tuttle, *op cit,* p. 832).

R.W. Wrangham, who is on the staff of the Center for Advanced Study in the Behavioral Sciences at Stanford University, says: "The dominant view today is that race is an outmoded concept" (Wrangham, *op cit,* p. 75). Similarly, Gould says: "Human variation exists; the formal designation of the races is passe" (Gould, *op cit,* p. 30).

For whatever it's worth, I myself have been
teaching and writing almost the same thing
about the race concept for over a quarter of a
century, at least 15 years in advance of the
modern school of anthropologists. This was not
because of any personal knowledge of human
genetics, which was minimal at best, but simply
because this was the teaching of Scripture.

MARXISM AND REVOLUTIONARY EVOLUTION

The youth rebellion of the sixties produced one
remarkable spin-off, the development of a strong
reaction against the older generation of scientists
as well as the older generation in general. This
meant, among other things, rebellion against the
Darwinist doctrine of slow-and-gradual evolution
in biology and the Lyellian doctrine of uniformitarianism in geology, with the recent graduates
in these fields preaching and promoting "quantum speciation" or "punctuated evolution" in
biology and "catastrophism" and "extinctionism"
in geology (note the further discussions in
Chapters IV-VI). This was partly because these
younger evolutionists had recognized the complete absence of scientific evidence for
Darwinian-type evolution which creationists had
been emphasizing for so long. But it was also
because the social implications of traditional
Darwinism (social Darwinism, racism, Nazism, imperialism, laissez-faire capitalism) were now being
repudiated in the name of left-wing evolutionism
(Marxism, communism, revolutionism). Commenting on these changes as they spilled over into the
field of physical anthropology, Matt
Cartmill says:

> "When people turn indignantly from one
> sort of speculation to embrace another,

> there are usually good, non-scientific
> reasons for it. . . . A myth, says my dic-
> tionary, is a real fictional story that
> embodies the cultural ideals of a people
> or expresses deep, commonly felt emo-
> tions. By this definition, myths are
> generally good things — and the origin
> stories that paleoanthropologists tell are
> necessarily myths" (*Natural History*, Vol.
> 92, November 1983, p. 77).

This recent conflict between the slow-and-
gradual (Darwinian) evolutionists and the
"punctuationist," revolutionary evolutionists,
with its overtones of the classic conflict between
the older generation and the younger generation,
as well as that between traditional "social-
Darwinist," laissez-faire, capitalistic economics
and environmentalist (neo-Lamarckian), neo-
catastrophist, Marxist economics, has been quite
bitter, especially in England and the United
States. The American controversy has focussed
especially at Harvard University, where two of
today's leading evolutionists, Dr. Stephen Jay
Gould and Dr. Edwin O. Wilson, have squared off
as the spokesmen for these two opposing schools
of evolutionary thought. Gould is the chief
American spokesman for "punctuated
equilibrium" and Wilson for "sociobiology," the
modern equivalent of traditional neo-Darwinism.
Reporting on this conflict, Dr. John Turner,
Reader in Evolutionary Genetics at the University
of Leeds, in England, says in a review article on
this situation:

> "It was the turn of E.O. Wilson and
> Richard Dawkins to be denounced, not
> this time from the pulpit as atheists, but

> by radical movements as fascist sym-
> pathizers. A Harvard group denounced
> Wilson's work as being in the intellectual
> tradition of Adolph Hitler" ("Why We
> Need Evolution by Jerks," *New Scientist*,
> Vol. 101; February 9, 1984, p. 34).

Richard Dawkins has already been mentioned
(p. 47) as the Oxford Professor who originated the
"selfish gene" theory. With reference to Gould,
Turner continues.

> "Stephen Gould, who has repeatedly
> urged the need to see man as essentially
> different from animals, and was one of
> the signatories of the 'Hitler' statement
> about E.O. Wilson, has found the answer
> in the punctuated equalibrium theory
> (*Ibid.*, p. 35).

Now, Wilson and Dawkins both vigorously deny
any connection with Nazism, as do their
followers, but there can be little doubt that, if
they were alive today, Hitler and Himmler and the
Nazi theoreticians would appropriate their
sociobiological arguments as further scientific
support for their Nazi racist and survival-of-the-
fittest philosophies. Dawkins and Wilson, of
course, are both doctrinaire atheists, although
Wilson testifies that he was once a Southern
Baptist fundamentalist, before encountering
evolutionary teachings as a student at the
University of Alabama (*The Humanist*, October
1982, p. 40).

Gould and his many followers may, as Turner
says, view man as distinct from animals, but this
is in a Marxist sense, not Biblical or creationist.
That is, *Homo sapiens* is believed to have

appeared suddenly — not by creation, but by an
evolutionary jerk, as Turner calls it. Gould is as
much an atheist as Wilson or Dawkins. In fact, he
is admittedly a Marxist, not a card-carrying communist, of course, but committed to the
philosophy and teachings of Karl Marx, which include atheism and evolutionism as foundational.

In commenting further on this latter-day conflict between these two schools of evolutionary
atheism, Turner makes the interesting admission
that neither is based on good scientific evidence.

> "Of the essential jerk theory, one can say
> as Gould did of sociobiology, that it
> brings no new insights, and can cite on
> its behalf not a single unambiguous fact.
>
> The point is not that the punctuated
> equilibrium theory is wrong. It might be
> right. The point is that despite its very
> poor scientific foundations it is attract-
> ing an enormous amount of attention.
> And as the Harvard radicals so cogently
> argued in the case of race and IQ, when
> an essentially meretricious scientific
> theory causes such a fuss, we must look
> to non-scientific causes" (John Turner,
> op cit., p. 35).

That is, both the neo-Darwinists (including
sociobiologists) and the punctuationists (reflect-
ing their Marxist tendencies) hold their views for
non-scientific reasons! Once again, as we have
been stressing in this chapter, evolution is not
science; it is always religion in one form
or another.

As bitterly opposed as they are to each other,
all these sects of evolutionism unite when con-
fronted with creationism, their common enemy.

And they especially hate *scientific* creationism, even though they must realize that they have no valid scientific proof or even good evidence for either slow evolution or sudden evolution. As bitter enemies of the true God and Biblical Christianity, they prefer anything to the truth of creation.

Now, commitment to evolution is nothing new for Marxism — whether the philosophical Marxism of the textbooks or the violent communism of the revolutionaries. All socialists, communists, anarchists, Leninists, Stalinists, Trotskyites, Maoists, Castroites, or whatever a particular school of Marxism or a particular Marxist national revolutionary movement may be called locally — all are founded upon evolutionism (whether Darwinian, Lamarckian, or some other brand) and atheism (even when it is called humanism or pantheism or something else).

It is time — high time, late time — for Christians to become alert to the fact that creationism is the only real antidote to this left-wing ideology that has already enslaved more than half the world and is now almost at our own gates. It is not only about to conquer the rest of the free world by revolution and military power, but even our own schools and other public institutions by its intellectual pretensions — all based on its atheistic evolutionary pseudo-scientific presuppositions.

Creationists are frequently criticized for saying that evolutionism is not merely a scientific concept but that it also has been the basis of anti-Christian social systems such as communism and socialism. Critics of creationism often express indignation when such supposedly unwarranted charges are made against evolutionary theory.

No creationist, of course, ever alleges that all evolutionists are atheists or communists. There are multitudes of both theistic evolutionists and evolutionary capitalists. However, it is a simple fact that evolutionary thinking is basic in socialism and communism and other such systems, whatever conclusion one wishes to draw from that fact. Socialistic and communistic writers frequently make a point of this, maintaining that this evolutionary structure proves their system to be "scientific."

For example, the famous periodical *International Socialist Review* (which includes a monthly supplement called its "Monthly Magazine Supplement to the Militant") in its November 1980 issue had as its feature article a lengthy attack on creationism entitled "Evolution vs. Creationism: In defense of Scientific Thinking," by Cliff Conner. Although the author exhibits only a very limited knowledge of creationist arguments and cites no creationist publication, he does attempt a rather sketchy summary of evidences for evolution, (including the long-discredited recapitulation theory!).

Of particular interest, however, is his concern that the creation movement may retard the advance of Marxism and socialism. Conner stresses the importance of evolution to these systems in such assertions as the following:

> "Defending Darwin is nothing new for socialists. The socialist movement recognized Darwinism as an important element in its general world outlook right from the start. When Darwin published his *Origin of Species* in 1859,

> Karl Marx wrote a letter to Frederick
> Engels in which he said: '. . . this is the
> book which contains the basis in natural
> history for our view.' "
>
> "By defending Darwinism, working
> people strengthen their defenses against
> the attacks of these reactionary outfits,
> and prepare the way for the transforma-
> tion of the social order."

Conner identifies himself and his colleagues as
"revolutionary socialists," whose aim is "as Marx
said: not merely to interpret the world but to
change it."

The article concludes with a testimony to
Darwin.

> "And of all those eminent researchers of
> the nineteenth century who have left us
> such a rich heritage of knowledge, we
> are especially grateful to Charles Darwin
> for opening our way to an evolutionary
> dialectical understanding of nature."

We suggest, therefore, that those theistic evolutionists and evolutionary capitalists who attack
creationists for suggesting an affinity between
evolutionism and socialism should concentrate
instead on attacking Marxists for suggesting this
same affinity. They started it!

We particularly need to be alert to the fact that
the modern shift by evolutionists to punctuated
equilibrium and catastrophism is not a move
toward Biblical creationism and flood geology, as
some might have hoped. If anything, it is even
more inimical (as a closer counterfeit) to true
creationism than was the old-style evolutionary
uniformitarianism. This new system is nothing

less than a very dangerous conditioning for revolution.

The older style Darwinian evolution, postulating the slow and gradual development of new species over millions of years, is rapidly being displaced by the idea that evolution proceeds in sudden jumps or revolutions. This theory of "punctuated equilibrium," introduced in 1972 and vigorously promoted by a vocal group of younger evolutionists under the leadership of Stephen Jay Gould, Harvard University's brilliant Marxist paleontologist, is rapidly taking over the schools.

The similarity of this type of evolutionary theory to Marxian revolutionary theory, which advocates social and economic evolution by intervals of intense revolution, is more than coincidental. The well-known gaps in the so-called fossil record, which actually give strong support to the special creation of each basic kind of organism, have been distorted to teach catastrophic evolution instead, and this concept in turn is used to support Marxist concepts of social change.

This evaluation is confirmed by one of England's leading evolutionists, Professor L.B. Halstead, who is himself (like Gould) an atheist, but who still believes in slow and gradual evolution. Writing in the leading science journal *Nature* (November 20, 1980, p. 208), he says:

> "This presents the public for the first time with the notion that there are no actual fossils directly antecedent to man ... (as) . . . the creationists have insisted on for years."

Halstead charges that these "saltatory evolutionists" are politically motivated, calling their theory "the recipe for revolution." He then makes an unexpected comparison:

> "Just as there are 'scientific' creationists seeking to falsify the concept of gradual change through time in favor of catastrophism, so too there are the Marxists who for different motives are equally concerned to discredit gradualism."

Actually there is no scientific evidence for either gradual evolution or rapid evolution. All the real facts of science conform precisely to the predictions of special creationism, exactly as taught in the Bible. Christians dare not settle for anything less than this, especially in their own Christian schools.

DARWIN AND MALE CHAUVINISM

The beleaguered Darwinian evolutionists have come under attack from another unexpected and unlikely quarter in recent years. Having already been labeled as racists and imperialists by the new wave of Marxian "revolutionary evolutionists," who insist that the old-style slow-and-gradual evolution must be replaced by rapid-and-catastrophic evolution, they have now been labeled as chauvinistic and sexist by radical feminists as well.

In a recent book entitled *Darwin,* Wilma George has attacked Charles Darwin's theories of the effect of "sexual selection" on human evolution as not having any basis in scientific fact at all, but as having been based on his Victorian prejudices against women and their abilities. Darwin's own wife, Emma, was quite religious and found her husband's anti-religious views very painful and his incessive hypochondria (which some writers maintain was a psychoneurosis related to his anti-religious guilt feelings) very demanding, but nevertheless was dutifully attentive and submissive to him throughout his life. Wilma George even shows that Darwin's insistence on an evolution-based male superiority was one major reason why he was able to get evolution so rapidly accepted in place of divine creation. Eveleen Richards comments:

> "In a period when women were beginning to demand the suffrage, higher education and entrance to middle-class professions, it was comforting to know that women could never outstrip men; the new Darwinism scientifically guaranteed it" (*New Scientist*, Vol. 100, December 22/29, 1983, p. 887). Darwinism supposedly proved female inferiority by ". . . an evolutionary reconstruction that centers on the aggressive, territorial, hunting male and relegates the female to submissive domesticity and the periphery of the evolutionary process" (*Ibid.*).

The feminist movement is not attacking evolution *per se*, of course, but only Darwinian-style evolution, just like the modern Marxist evolutionists are doing.

In any case, Charles Darwin, once considered such a great man and great scientist, is rapidly becoming little more than a fallen idol today, even to those who paid devoted homage to him just a few years ago.

Christian women should not be deceived by the radical feminist movement today, although

women in these movements do have some
legitimate complaints against a social system
that still reflects in considerable degree the social
Darwinism of the post-Darwin century as well as
the evolutionary pantheism of both ancient and
modern non-Christian religions and philosophies.
They should remember that *all* of these other
religious systems have relegated women to a very
inferior place in society. As already pointed out,
all such religions are fundamentally evolutionary
philosophies of one sort or another.

The Bible, on the other hand, has never taught
male "superiority," though it does delineate the
distinctive divine purposes for men and women (a
subject well beyond the scope of this brief discussion). As far as "equal rights" are concerned, in
terms of real eternal values, men and women
have always been equal before God — equal in
creation and equal in salvation.

> "So God created man in his own image,
> in the image of God created he him;
> male and female created he them"
> (Genesis 1:27).
>   "...there is neither male nor female;
> for ye are all one in Christ Jesus"
> (Galatians 3:28).

The real answer to the unresolved needs and
problems of women in our society is an all-out
commitment to genuine Biblical creationism.

"CHRISTIAN" EVOLUTIONISM

In view of the foundational importance of creationism to Biblical Christianity, as emphasized in
Chapter I, and the deadly effects of evolutionism
as a socio-religious philosophy, as demonstrated
in this chapter, it would seem obvious that all

true Christians should abhor and oppose evolution with great vigor. The tragic truth is, however,
that most professing Christians have either compromised with evolution or have been indifferent
to its vital importance.

The so-called Christian "liberals" who control
practically all the main-line denominations have
long since accepted evolution. One could perhaps
expect this, since such liberal theologians have
also rejected Biblical inerrancy. A great problem
is that many neo-evangelicals and conservatives
have also accepted theistic evolution. Even many
fundamentalists, who do sincerely believe in
special creation and reject evolution, consider the
issue as more or less secondary in importance
and say little about it.

Consequently, the testimony of the Christian
church against evolutionism has been relatively
ineffectual ever since Darwin. There have been
significant exceptions to this pattern, of course,
but these occasional exceptions have not been
enough to stem the tide of evolutionary thought.

It is acknowledged, of course, that most evolutionists are not atheistic humanists (though most
of the spokesmen and leaders of evolutionary
thought seem to be). The typical layman's view of
evolution is that it somehow constitutes God's
method of creation and, therefore, should be of
no great concern to Christians. A great many
"born-again" Christians would, if pressed, admit
to being "theistic evolutionists."

Creationists, however, have long maintained
that theistic evolution is actually a contradiction
in terms, like "Christian atheism." If evolution is
able to explain all forms of life, as leading evolutionists insist, then God is redundant. Furthermore, the very essence of evolution is one of

chance variations, waste, inefficiency, struggle
and survival or extinction. The very terms are inconsistent with a God of wisdom and power, and
with the ethics of Christianity. Such considerations, however, are often ignored, especially when
they are pointed out by Biblical fundamentalists.

It is therefore doubly significant when this
same fact is pointed out by a leading scientific
atheistic evolutionist such as Jacques Monod. On
a broadcast interview in Australia shortly before
his death, this outstanding, Nobel Prize-winning
French biologist, author of the influential book
Chance and Necessity, said (as reported in the
Australian creationist journal *Ex Nihilo*) concerning the evolutionary process:

> "Why would God have to have chosen
> this extremely complex and difficult
> mechanism? . . . Why not create man
> right away, as of course classical
> religions believed?"

Monod, of course, had opted for belief in
complete naturalism and atheism, driven to this
position by the inexorable logic of what he considered to be the indubitable "fact" of evolution.
He said, further:

> "[Natural] selection is the blindest, and
> most cruel way of evolving new species,
> . . . The struggle for life and elimination
> of the weakest is a horrible process,
> against which our whole modern ethics
> revolts. An ideal society is a nonselective
> society, one where the weak is protected;
> which is exactly the reverse of the so-
> called natural law. I am surprised that a
> Christian would defend the idea that this

> is the process which God more or less
> set up in order to have evolution."

If an atheist is surprised that a Christian would defend evolution, what must be the attitude of God Himself toward such a compromising viewpoint, which not only rejects the plain teaching of God's Word but also maligns His character?

Christians who have been indifferent to the menace of evolution should consider the following analysis by Dr. William Provine, who is both Professor of History and Professor of Biological Sciences at Cornell University.

> "As Jacques Monod, E.O. Wilson, and many other biologists have pointed out, modern evolutionary biology has shattered the hope that some kind of designing or purposive force guided human evolution and established the basis of moral rules. Instead, biology leads to a wholly mechanistic view of life. . . There are no gods and no designing forces. The frequently made assertion that modern biology and assumptions of the Judeo-Christian tradition are fully compatible is false. Second, there exist no inherent moral or ethical laws, no absolute guiding principles for human society." ("Influence of Darwin's Ideas on the Study of Evolution," *Bioscience,* Vol. 32, June 1982, p. 506.)

If Provine and all his humanistic colleagues are right (that is, if evolution is true), then Christianity (or any other theistic religion) is redundant, or even harmful.

> "Religion is like the human appendix:

> although it was functionial in our distant
> ancestors, it is of no use today. Just as
> the appendix today is a focus of physical
> disease, so too religion today is a focus
> of social disease. Although religion was a
> force accelerating human evolution
> during the Ice Age, it is now an atavism
> of negative value." (Frank R. Zindler,
> "Religion, Hypnosis and Music: An Evolu-
> tionary Perspective," *American Atheist*,
> Vol. 26, October 1984, p. 24).

The above opinion is that of the former chair-
man of the division of science and technology at
one of the colleges of the State University of New
York. He is currently a most vociferous anti-
creationist activist. In any case, his conclusion is
quite sound if his premise is valid. That is, if
evolution is true, then the Christian religion is
false and, for the good of further evolutionary
progress, the sooner it can be forgotten,
the better.

But, thankfully, evolution is *not* true! As will be
shown in Part II, the real facts of science support
Biblical creationism and the entire Biblical
revelation. The entire premise and framework of
evolutionism is altogether false and its impact in
human life and thought has been devastatingly
harmful. Christians urgently need to become
informed and concerned and active in the battle
to rebuild Biblical creationism as the foundation
of all truth and life.

The main purpose of this book, Lord willing, is
to enlist many more Christians as convinced,
committed and aggressive creationists. As will be
shown in the next chapter, a critical battle
between these two world views is already under

way and it will surely become more extensive and intensive as time goes on. It is urgent that as many Christians as possible be prepared, alert and active in this most important battle.

Chapter III

Evolutionism in The Last Days

THE BATTLE AGAINST CREATION

In the first chapter of this book, it was shown that the doctrine of God as omnipotent transcendent Creator, with the universe as the direct effect of His purposeful, special, recent creative acts, as revealed and recorded in His inerrant and fully perspicuous Scriptures, is of paramount importance to true faith and meaningful life. Then, the inescapable fallacies and the evil results of the opposing cosmogony, that of evolutionary humanism, along with the dangers of any Christian compromise therewith, were demonstrated in Chapter 2. The three chapters in Part II will provide a survey of the relevant scientific data, all of which tend to confirm the Biblical record of creation and primeval history while clearly refuting the evolution model, showing that there is certainly no need for the Christian to be intimidated into silence or compromise by evolutionist propaganda.

In view of the cosmic and age-long proportions of the cosmic conflict, it is inevitable that it will become more and more severe as this present age draws to a close. The Bible, of course, in-

dicates that the Lord Jesus Christ, as Creator and
Redeemer of the world, must eventually put down
all rebellion and then reign as undisputed
Sovereign of His creation for ever and ever.
Humanists, on the other hand, convinced that the
Bible is false and that there is no Creator at all,
predict the imminent demise of all theistic
religions, especially Biblical Christianity, and are
working hard to achieve the fulfillment of this
goal. In any event, this conflict of the ages will
continue and intensify as time goes on, and
Christians urgently need to be informed
and ready.

THE ANTI-CREATIONISTS

An amazing development has been under way
in the academic world since about 1980. Many
meetings have been called, committees are being
formed everywhere, plans of action devised and
alarms sounded up and down the land. The
academic establishment is being supported in
this crusade by all the power of the news media,
with editorial columnists, news commentators
and ordinary reporters all being enlisted to help
turn back a bold assault on the citadels of
supposed wisdom and learning.

Who is this fearsome foe against which such
unprecedented defenses must be erected? Is it
the Marxists? The pornographers? The occultists?
No, of course not! Academic freedom must be
preserved, so such groups as these must all be
accommodated and defended, not opposed.

It is the creationists! *This* movement *must* be
stopped, at all costs. Professor Delos B. McKown,
Head of Auburn University's Philosophy Department, formerly a preacher and now a self-
appointed defender of the scientific establishment,

has solemnly proclaimed the following.

> ". . . old time religion (is) something that educated people, both believers and nonbelievers, had thought was safely behind us in the old times, where it belongs. But, alas, modern, scientific, progressive America is witnessing a reactivation of biblical literalism, fundamentalism, and evangelicalism that almost defies belief. . . . But, of all the recent manifestations of old-time religion, I can think of none more impertinent than that of the Institute for Creation Research, which is devoted to destroying the ideas of cosmic and organic evolution. The mischief this organization is prepared to do to the life and earth sciences in elementary and secondary schools defies the scientific imagination" ("Contemporary Religion versus Science," *Chemtech*, June 1981, p. 336).

Dr. McKown is only one of a growing host of such alarmists today, and probably not a very important one at that. Much more imposing is the array of scientific and educational bodies that have organized for an all-out battle against teaching the concept of creation in the public schools. Among other actions, the prestigious National Academy of Sciences, in October 1981, called a meeting of leading scientists and educators in Washington to discuss ways of dealing with those who oppose evolutionism. The next day a similar meeting was sponsored by the National Association of Biology Teachers.

The largest and most influential scientific

organization, the American Association for Advancement of Science, has held many councils, as well as lecture sessions at its conventions, and has published a long series of critical articles on creationism in its journals. Local Committees of Correspondence have been formed in practically every state, their function being to combat creationism wherever it surfaces at the local level.

It is almost refreshing, in fact, to hear the cries of alarm that are being sounded these days against creationists. Humanistic leaders of the giant evolutionary establishment, after decades of ridiculing biblical creation, are now becoming almost hysterically afraid of losing their long-held control of the nation's educational systems to what they claim is an insignificant "fundamentalist fringe."

The gigantic American Association for the Advancement of science, for example, most powerful of all scientific organizations, views creationism with great fear. "We are very concerned about creationism," states William Carey, executive officer of AAAS, "and it was the subject of long discussion at our recent board meeting" ("A Response to Creationism Evolves," *Science,* Vol. 214, November 6, 1981, p. 638). Evolutionists are especially afraid of participating in scientific debates on evolution versus creation. "All but one voice at the NAS (National Academy of Sciences) gathering agreed that debating with creationists should be avoided" (*Ibid.,* p. 635). Instead, AAAS arranged for 100,000 free copies of a special anti-creationist diatribe in the December issue of its popular magazine *Science 81* to be given to the nation's science teachers. This particular tract closes with the following distress call: "What is at stake is how the people of the

United States look at science in the next decades and what they teach their children."

Similarly, the National Association of Biology Teachers established a regular mini-journal devoted primarily to opposing creationism. In the October, 1981, issue of this journal (arrogantly named *Scientific Integrity* — a better name would be *Scientific Sophistry!*), NABT Executive Secretary Wayne Moyer says that a national "communications network" of local committees has been set up to "support grassroots efforts in meeting the challenge of creationism." The American Civil Liberties Union brought in a battery of New York lawyers and a parade of big-name scientists to buttress its lawsuits against creationism in Arkansas and Louisiana.

The list of organizations that have become active in the fight against the Creator goes on and on — the American Humanist Association, the American Civil Liberties Union, the National Science Teachers Association, the American Geological Institute (incorporating all the societies in the geological field), the American Chemical Society, the National Educators Assocation, the American Institute of Biological Sciences, the American Anthropological Association, and many others.

Some of the proposals and action plans emanating from these various deliberations were the following: (1) publish and distribute numerous books, articles, and pamphlets criticizing creationists and creationism; (2) *don't* participate in any more creation-evolution debates with creationists scientists if they can be avoided; (3) help prepare and support the most appropriate debaters when debates are unavoidable; (4) organize an Institute for Evolu-

tion Research "to counter the San Diego-based
Institute for Creation Research"; (5) develop a
national consortium of organizations united to
fight creation; (6) develop a strong program of
political action to lobby legislatures, departments
of education and school boards; (7) initiate a
nationwide series of short courses, designed to
equip teachers to promote the evolutionist position in their classes; (8) prepare evolution television specials for broadcast on P.B.S. and other
outlets; (9) try to get every scientist and science
teacher to contribute $10 annually for the work
of the consortium.

The above are only a few of the many suggestions developed at these meetings. Some of these,
along with many others, were presented at the
National Academy meeting in a paper "Countering
the Creationists" by long-time anti-creationist
John A. Moore, biologist at the University of
California at Riverside. Dr. Moore made a very
important point in conclusion:

> "If we do not resolve our problems with
> the creationists, we have only ourselves
> to blame. Let's remember, the greatest
> resource of all is available to us — the
> educational system of the nation."

Evolutionists, unfortunately, *do* seem to control
our educational system, as well as our courts and
news media today, and all these resources are being mobilized to do battle with the fearful
menace of creation!

Somehow the term "overkill" comes to mind.
According to the conventional wisdom, creationists are an insignificant fundamentalist sect,
and scientific creationism, according to Harvard's
Stephen Jay Gould, is merely a "nonsense term."

There would be a much simpler, quicker and less expensive way to stop the creation movement, of course, but none of these evolutionary strategists seem to have thought of it. All they would have to do would be to provide one single documented *proof* of evolution, or even a few unequivocal scientific evidences!

In the meantime, there is another word that also comes to mind — *"Why?" "Why* do the . . . people imagine a vain thing? . . . (taking) counsel together against the Lord, . . . saying, Let us break their bands asunder, and cast away their cords from us" (Psalm 2:1-3). If evolution is such an assured fact of science and creation is scientific nonsense, why are they so afraid of allowing young people to evaluate the facts for themselves? On the other hand, if there could indeed be a Creator, and if He really could have created this universe, it is sad and foolish for educators to withhold this vital information from the young people whose training has been committed into their hands. The founding fathers of our nation, those who wrote the Declaration of Independence and the Bill of Rights, certainly never intended such a thing.

THE GROWING MENACE OF HUMANISM

The atheist, John Dunphy, in a prize-winning humanist eassay, has very perceptively outlined the coming battle for the minds of young people in the following call to arms:

> "I am convinced that the battle for humankind's future must be waged and won in the public school classroom by teachers who correctly perceive their role as the proselytizers of a new faith: a religion of humanity that respects the

spark of what theologians call divinity in
every human being. These teachers must
embody the same selfless dedication as
the most rabid fundamentalist
preachers, for they will be ministers of
another sort, utilizing a classroom
instead of a pulpit to convey humanist
values in whatever subject they teach,
regardless of the educational level —
preschool day care or large state university. The classroom must and will
become an arena of conflict between the
old and the new — the rotting corpse of
Christianity, together with all its adja-
cent evils and misery, and the new faith
of humanism, resplendent in its promise
of a world in which the never-realized
Christian ideal of 'love thy neighbor' will
finally be achieved" (John J. Dunphy, "A
Religion for a New Age," *The Humanist,*
January/February 1983, p. 26).

Such declarations of spiritual warfare and
words of blasphemy are coming thick and fast
these days. Of special significance was the 1980
"Secular Humanist Declaration." This document
was published in the first issue of a new
humanist magazine mis-named *Free Inquiry,* and
it was reported in the *New York Times* as follows:

"A group of 58 prominent scholars and
writers have attacked the recent rise in
Christian fundamentalism by issuing a
declaration that denounces absolutist
morality and calls for a emphasis on
science and reason rather than religion
as a means of solving human problems. ...

> Reflecting elements of two earlier
> humanist manifestors, in 1933 and
> 1973, the declaration depicts super-
> natural religion and divine revelation as
> enemies of the rational process that
> leads to progress' (As reported in *New
> York Times*, October 15, 1980).

The signers of this document included Isaac
Asimov, Sir Francis Crick, Albert Ellis, B.F. Skinner,
Joseph Fletcher, Ernest Nagel, Milovan Djilas,
Baroness Barbara Wootton, Sidney Hook, and
many other such notables. Editor of the magazine
is Dr. Paul Kurtz. Although many humanists profess high ideals and have endorsed many virtues
and goals which are also cherished by Christians,
their fundamental premises are those of atheism
and evolution, and these poisoned roots inevitably generate corrupt fruits, as documented
in Chapter II.

The Humanist Manifestos I and II, referred to in
the above quotation, have received considerable
attention in recent years, both by Christian fundamentalists and secular humanists, so they are
now rather well known. It is significant that one
of the main founders and leaders of this more or
less "official" modern humanist movement was
John Dewey, who was largely responsible for both
the original Manifesto and the organizing of the
American Humanist Association in the early
1940s. Dewey, of course, is universally recognized
as the chief architect of the modern system of
"progressive education," the person most influential in leading American public schools into the
humanistic quagmire in which they have been
floundering for over half a century.

HUMANISM AND THE DRIVE FOR
WORLD GOVERNMENT

Almost as influential as Dewey was another "founding father" of modern secular humanism, Sir Julian Huxley, the first Director-General of UNESCO and the world's most prominent evolutionist spokesman during the first half of the 20th century. The original "Framework" which he proposed for UNESCO, right after World War II when the United Nations Organization was established, was kept more-or-less "in-house" for a long time, but was finally published in *The Humanist* magazine in 1979. The following typical excerpts indicate the tenor of this profoundly anti-Christian document:

> "Thus the general philosophy of UNESCO should, it seems, be a scientific world humanism, global in extent and evolutionary in background" ("A New World Vision," *The Humanist,* Vol. XXXIX, March/April 1979, p. 35).
>
> "Thus the struggle for existence that underlies natural selection is increasingly replaced by conscious selection, a struggle between ideas and values in consciousness" (*Ibid.,* p. 36).
>
> "The unifying of traditions into a single common pool of experience, awareness, and purpose is the necessary prerequisite for further major progress in human evolution. Accordingly, although political unification in some sort of world government will be required for the definitive attainment of this stage, unification in the things of the mind is not only necessary also, but it can pave

the way for other types of unification"
(*Ibid.*, p. 38).

Thus, Huxley was advocating in this proposal
not only a world government, but also a world
educational system, controlled social evolution,
and a world religious system, all based on secular
evolutionary humanism. He exerted profound
influence, especially among scientists and
educators, as well as political leaders all over the
world, for well over half a century. And,
significantly, he was an outspoken atheist and
bitter enemy of any theistic religion, especially
Biblical Christianity.

Huxley's involvement in both humanism and
evolutionism was no accident, since these two
belief systems are essentially identical. The very
first tenet of the first Humanist Manifesto (1933)
is a statement of faith in the naturalistic evolutionary origin of the universe. The second tenet is
a statement of faith in the naturalistic evolutionary origin of man (see pp. 66-68). On these
two beliefs "hang all the law and the prophets"
of humanism.

Huxley was the grandson of Thomas Huxley,
who had been known as "Darwin's bulldog" in the
early days of Darwinism. Julian Huxley and his
brother Aldous (known for his advocacy of
"sexual freedom" and as the chief founding pro-
pagator of the modern drug culture) were, like
their grandfather, bitter in their hatred of the
Christian religion and the Christian clergy.
Thomas had called himself an "agnostic" but
both Julian and Aldous boasted that they were
atheists.

Sir Julian was the most influential evolutionist
of the first half of the twentieth century, probably

chief founder and advocate of what came to be known as "neo-Darwinism" or "the modern evolutionary synthesis." He was keynote speaker at the famous Darwinian Centennial Convocation at the University of Chicago in 1959. But probably his greatest impact was as UNESCO's first Director-General. His influence on American humanism as a signatory of the first Humanist Manifesto and a founder of the American Humanist Association, has been incalculable.

It is not surprising that Tenets 13 and 14 of the Manifesto, in effect urge that society be united around a common world religion of humanism, and that all nations be united in a common world government, whose description is essentially the same as that of socialistic communism. UNESCO and other United Nations organizations, as well as multitudes of other organizations today are steadily working toward such goals. It is urgent that concerned Americans — especially Bible-believing Christians — recognize and remember the fact that the evolutionary philosophy is at the root of all this.

FALSE TEACHERS

Many Christian organizations have become very exercised, and rightly so, about such issues as abortion and pornography, racism and communism, and in trying to win or reclaim those entrapped in such sins as homosexuality or drug use. All this is good and necessary, but nevertheless it is not getting at the root of the problem. To keep the weeds out of the garden, the seeds must be purged from the ground. Corrupt roots produce corrupt fruits. The seeds and the roots of all these evils constitute nothing less

than the age-long evolutionist world view, which
expressed itself in former ages in various forms
of pantheistic polytheism, in the post-Darwinian
century as naturalistic gradualistic "scientific"
evolutionism, and which now seems to be changing
into a revolutionary evolutionism and, in some
quarters at least, returning again to pantheistic
mysticism — all of which are implacably opposed
to true creationism and Biblical
Christianity.

EVOLUTIONIST CONTROL IN THE SCHOOLS

Significantly, these enemies of God have cun-
ningly chosen the most effective battlefield for
this conflict of the ages. Although they are active
on many fronts, the key campaigns have been
and are being waged in the schools. They feel
that if they can win the minds of even a single
generation (and this can be done most effectively
when those minds are young and plastic and inclined to be naturally rebellious against the older
generation anyhow), they will win the war and
defeat God once and for all.

So it should not be too surprising when we find
evolution at the foundation of practically every
subject now being taught in our public schools.
The evolutionary origin of life and the various
forms of life is the key theme of all courses in the
life sciences. The evolution of the universe and of
the chemical elements begins all courses in the
physical sciences. The evolutionary "ages" of
geology form the interpretive framework of the
earth sciences. The animalistic origin of man and
all his social systems are basic in anthropology,
psychology, sociology, economics, history and all
the other social sciences, with evolution being
even more systematically applied in these fields

than in the natural sciences. Even in the
humanities and fine arts, the many themes of
humanism are prominent.

For the most part, Bible-believing Christians
still seem either uninformed or unconcerned
about all this, but the times are perilous and the
hour is late. Too many Christians consider creationism to be a somewhat unimportant issue that
might concern a few specialists but which is not
really vital to the Christian life.

On the other hand, evolutionary humanists *do*
recognize its vital importance. This is why they
become so hysterical at the very mention of
scientific creationism and why they are so intrac-
tably opposed to allowing students to learn
anything about it at all. They have finally obtained
almost complete control of the public schools
and of the minds of the nation's young people,
and they know that true scientific Biblical creationism could easily destroy all their gains.

These gains are the product of almost 200
years of diligent subversion, especially through
the efforts of such men as the rationalist/
socialist/spiritualist, Robert Owen (1771-1858),
the Unitarian Horace Mann (1796-1859), the
radical humanist John Dewey (1859-1952), and
all their colleagues and disciples. They were able
gradually to transform the nation's original
schools, which were soundly creationist, Biblical
and church controlled, first into a system of
"common schools," then into a system of state-
controlled schools with teachers prepared by
state-controlled teachers' colleges, and finally
into the temples of evolutionary humanism which
we have today. See Samuel L. Blumenfeld, *Is
Public Education Necessary?* (Old Greenwich, CT,
Devin-Adair Co., 1981, 263 pp.) for a fascinating

and well-documented discussion of the history of the atheistic and anti-Christian background of the development of American public schools in the early 19th century.

Although most people — even most Christians — seem to remain indifferent to this situation, there are at least some stirrings that may lead to an awakening. Marshall Foster comments:

> "There is no doubt, though, that we are at present intellectually unprepared for the battle. The ACLU's attacks on our Biblical base as a nation are only the tip of an iceberg of hatred toward God and his believers that is sweeping the world. But we as Americans share a heritage from God that is unprecedented. Millions of us are now awakening to this heritage, and this is the beginning of a potential Great Awakening" ("Christian Offensive or Secular Checkmate?" *Mayflower Institute Journal,* Vol. 1, July/August 1983, p. 3).

Foster also notes that at least the first 24 state constitutions of the United States recognized Biblical Christianity as the quasi-established religion of their communities (*Ibid.,* p. 1). He also reminds us that, during the Revolutionary War, Congress itself imported 20,000 Bibles for use by the people and in 1782 passed a resolution recommending the first Bible actually published in America (*Ibid.,* p. 2).

Now, on the other hand, not only are the Bible and sound Christian literature banned from our classrooms, creationist books — even those which are strictly scientific in content and emphasis — are being purged from school libraries!

One of the most ominous indications of a developing Orwellian-type "double-think" or "newspeak" syndrome is the widespread charge that creationists are trying to "censor" the textbooks and teachers in the public schools. The truth, of course, is the exact opposite. It is the evolutionary humanists who are the censors.

The best-known example is the notorious Arkansas "creation trial" of 1981, where the wrath of the nation's intellectual establishment was brought down on those well-meaning citizens who desired their schools merely to include the scientific creationist alternative (along with evolution) in the teachings received by their children. The result was a smashing victory for the so-called American Civil Liberties Union, and a further entrenchment of the state-established religion of humanism in their own schools. The widely published ACLU threat to file a similar suit against any state or school district that authorizes a "two-model" approach in their schools has so intimidated authorities that the public schools are now effectively closed to any hint of creationism in their textbooks.

But that is not all. The same is true of school libraries, so the students and teachers cannot even read creationist literature on their own time. Many surveys have shown that the typical high school library is well stocked with books on evolution, as well as books on religion (that is, on liberal religion, Eastern religions, occult religions, and the like), but has only two or three creationist books, if any. This is also the case with public libraries.

Furthermore, even when creationist books are donated to a library, and accepted by the library, the chances are they won't stay there long. A recent correspondent tells how he donated $200 worth of ICR books to his local library, only to find after a few weeks that they had all mysteriously disappeared!

And even that isn't all. The Creation-Life Publishers have made diligent efforts to get ICR books sold through secular book stores, in airport newstands and various other public places (including national and state parks, where evolutionist books are available in abundance), only to be perpetually rebuffed. It's hard even to get Christian book stores to carry them!

We could cite many other examples of this pervasive humanist-orchestrated blackout of the great truth of divine creation. The priests of evolutionary humanistic pantheism/atheism effectively control public education, the news media, and the government bureaucracies, and they intend for it to stay that way.

But so far they don't control our homes! If children are going to be brainwashed in the public schools, it becomes more important than ever for concerned parents to support Christian schools or other private schools where God is at least recognized as Creator and Sovereign. Furthermore, sound home teaching is vital — possibly in some cases even full-time home schooling. Even though creationist books are rejected by the public schools, they can still be very effectively used by parents to help teach their own children.

The American nation, genuine science, and Biblical religion were all built on a creationist foundation. But, "if the foundations be destroyed, what can the righteous do?" (Psalm 11:3).

Even President Ronald Reagan has expressed

similar concerns, including a concern over the
banning of God from the public schools.

> "God, the source of our knowledge, has
> been expelled from the classroom. He
> gives us His great blessing: life . . . and
> yet many would condone the taking of
> innocent life. We expect Him to protect
> us in a crisis, but turn away from Him
> too often in our day-to-day living. And I
> wonder if He isn't waiting for us to wake
> up" (Address at National Prayer
> Breakfast, in Washington D.C., 1982).

The awakening which the President would
encourage is most urgently and critically needed
in the minds and souls of our young people, and
this requires directing their thoughts back to the
reality of special creation and a Creator to whom
all are responsible. But this means that
Christians must somehow be awakened to
the need.

THE PROBLEM OF CHRISTIAN INDIFFERENCE

The only reason that the early schools of the
nation could be taken over by the unitarians and
secularists back in the early nineteenth century,
and then transformed into statist institutions
with a least-common-denominator humanistic
religious philosophy by the twentieth century,
was the compromising indifference of the
religious leaders of the period, as Blumenfeld's
book (mentioned on p. 112) makes abundantly
clear. This was also the case with the triumph of
Darwinian-style evolutionism in the last half of
the nineteenth century.

Most people have the impression that the
religionists of Darwin's day opposed evolutionism

while the scientists promoted it, with the resulting conflict being a classic example of religious bigotry opposing science, but it was really the other way around. The original and most vigorious opposition to Darwin came from scientists, whereas many religious leaders were ready to accommodate "evolution" right from the start. As Francis Glasson says:

> "Darwin expected that his book would arouse violent criticism from the scientific world, and it certainly came from that quarter. According to his own account, most of the leading scientists of the day believed in the immutability of species. . . . On the other hand, many Christian leaders took a very different line, even from the early stages; . . . . Owen Chadwick, Regius Professor of Modern History at Cambridge, wrote after extensive research: 'At first much of the opposition to Darwin's theory came from scientists on grounds of evidence, not from theologians on grounds of Scripture' " ("Darwin and the Church," *New Scientist,* Vol. 99, September 1, 1983, pp. 638, 639).

The same has been true ever since, and is certainly true today. Almost all college and seminary faculty members of the large denominations teach theistic evolution and most of the faculty members of the so-called evangelical colleges and seminaries today teach the compromise view known euphemistically as "progressive creation." Even many professors in the "fundamentalist" schools and churches teach the "gap theory," thinking thereby to avoid the problem, placing the supposed evolutionary ages of earth history in an imaginary gap between the first two verses of Genesis.

Consequently, the modern creationist revival has been brought about primarily through the efforts of creationist scientists, as well as many concerned lay men and women in various fields. Although there are many exceptions, the religious establishment has, if anything, been even more adamant in its opposition to true creationism than the practicing scientists. This has been especially true of liberal and neo-evangelical theologians.

But probably the most disappointing aspect of the modern situation is not the overt opposition of humanists and religious liberals (this was to be expected) but the general apathy of Bible-believing Christians everywhere, those who profess belief in Biblical inerrancy and all the doctrines of the Gospel. Somehow these Christian people need to be informed and mobilized, not only to witnessing for Christ, or even to fighting social evils, but to the vital necessity of restoring creationism to its primary place in the thinking of our nation and its people.

Unless this can be done, the public schools (and, therefore, the coming generation) seem irretrievably lost. For a while it did seem that creationism might be restored to these schools in some measure — not Biblical creationism, of course, but scientific creationism, on a "two-model" basis. As admitted by D.J. Futuyma, who has written one of the many anti-creationist books published recently:

> "Creation and evolution, between them, exhaust the possible explanations for the

origin of living things. Organisms either appeared on the earth fully developed or they did not. If they did not, they must have developed from pre-existing species by some process of modification. If they did appear in a fully developed state, they must indeed have been created by some omnipotent intelligence" (*Science on Trial,* Pantheon Books, 1983, p. 197).

This is exactly what creationist scientists claim also. They propose that the two models of origins be examined scientifically and objectively in textbooks and classrooms, giving arguments and evidences for each, without reference to the Bible or any religious arguments, leaving the students to decide for themselves what to believe. That creationism *can* be taught in this manner, quite effectively, can be ascertained from numerous books prepared for this purpose (For example, see the ICR books *Scientific Creationism* and *What is Creation Science?*).

This two-model approach is eminently fair and reasonable, in accordance with good teaching techniques, academic freedom and civil rights. It promotes no particular denomination or religion and is neither illegal nor contrary to any provision in either state or federal constitutions.[1]

Nevertheless the humanistic establishments in science and education would have none of it, and they were supported in their opposition by large

---

1. For a book specifically designed for use in public schools, see *How to Teach Origins without ACLU Interference,* by John N. Moore (Mott Media, 1984, 382 pp.)

numbers of religious leaders as well. Wherever adopted in any fashion on a statewide basis, the two-model approach has been thrown out on one pretext or another (Tennessee, Indiana, Arkansas, Louisiana, Texas) by the courts or attorneys general. The American Humanist Association and the American Civil Liberties Union are leading the fight against creation-science everywhere, and have threatened to oppose it by every means possible wherever it appears in a local school district. A national network of statewide and local Committees on Correspondence has been established to spearhead the anti-creationist fight at the local level.

At least 30 anti-creationist books have been published in recent years, plus hundreds and hundreds of articles. Anti-creationist sessions have been held in scores of scientific, educational and religious conventions and other meetings. Creationist scientists have been slandered, their writings have been distorted and almost always quoted out of context, their arguments have been misrepresented, and everything possible done to discredit them in the minds of the public.

All of this has, indeed, been enough to intimidate most Christians. Many of these believe in creationism and would be active supporters if it were popular but, under the circumstances, they prefer to keep at a safe distance from the fray. Consequently, our public schools get worse and worse.

A RETURN
TO TRUE CHRISTIAN EDUCATION

Although Christians dare not ignore the millions of young people who need help in the public schools, and must continue to try in every way feasible to restore true creationism back to its rightful place in these schools and also to correct their humanistic, anti-Christian biases wherever possible, there is no doubt that the most satisfying and fruitful process of education can only be implemented through Christian schools and/or home schools. The burgeoning growth of Bible-centered Christian schools and colleges is just about the only encouraging sign in the educational field these days, and the movement should be supported in every way possible.

Nearly all of the new Christian schools are solidly creationist in their position, although their commitment to true Biblical (recent, literal, six-day) creation and the Noahic global flood is too often somewhat soft and equivocal. Their faculties and administration may still be intimidated by their own educational backgrounds, which often were in neo-evangelical schools and in the graduate programs of the humanistic state universities.

Despite such problems, the Christian school movement is alive and well, growing stronger both numerically and academically, as well as doctrinally. It is hoped these schools will all try to develop all their courses and curricula within the constraining framework of Scripture, especially in the key areas of origins and history. Since this is the true Biblical norm for education, this should be far more effective in training and equipping young people than the public schools with their humanistic indoctrination. A comprehensive exposition and analysis of these Biblical criteria for true education can be found in my book, *Education for the Real World* (Master Books, 1983, 285 pp.).

Certainly nothing is lost of true educational value this way. It is not science, for example, that is either anti-Christian or a-Christian, but scientism. The actual facts of science fully support creationism and the full Biblical record. In fact, modern science is itself a direct outgrowth of the Biblical world view. Colin Russell has recently supported this contention as follows:

> "Thus some Victorian writers, intoxicated with the idea of progress . . . rewrote the history of science in terms of a conflict between science and religion . . . Today historical justification for that position is amazingly hard to justify. It is widely accepted on all sides that, far from undermining it, science is deeply indebted to Christianity and has been so from at least the scientific revolution. Recent historical research has uncovered many unexpected links between scientific enterprise and Biblical theology. The 'conflict' model is not just a harmless anachronism. It is truth standing on its head" (*Nature,* Vol. 308, April 26, 1984, p. 777).

Similar statements could be multiplied. Another scientific historian, George M. Marsden, professor at Calvin College in Michigan, admits:

> "The American folk epistemology, then, is by no means anti-scientific in principle. Rather it is based on a naive realism plus popular mythology concerning proper scientific procedure and vertifica-tion. These procedures are essentially Baconian, favoring simple empirical

evidence" (*Nature*, Vol. 305, October 15, 1983, p. 573).

The "American folk epistemology" is Marsden's patronizing term for straightforward Biblical creationism. He thus admits the latter is scientific in principle, based on naive realism and in accord with the sound experimental procedure of Bacon's universally accepted scientific method. By inference, therefore, evolutionism is "sophisticated unrealism," accepted without proper scientific verification. Interestingly enough, although Marsden teaches at a purportedly Christian college, he still served as a witness for the evolutionists at the Arkansas creation "trial."

In any case, genuine science is certainly compatible with creationism and the Bible, fully appropriate for teaching in a Christian school setting. The same is true for all other disciplines. Just as evolutionism has been made the false foundation and framework for the various disciplines in the public schools, so Biblical creationism, conservationism and consummationism (Colossians 1:16-20) can be taken as the true and satisfying framework for these disciplines in the Christian school. Marsden makes another interesting and important admission in this connection:

> "In any case, creation scientists are correct in perceiving that in modern culture 'evolution' often involves far more than biology. The basic ideologies of the civilization, including its entire moral structure, are at issue. Evolution is sometimes the key mythological element in a philosophy that functions as

a virtual religion. . . . Dogmatic
proponents of evolutionary anti-
supernaturalistic mythologies have been
inviting responses in kind" (*Ibid.,*
p. 574).

Thus, since evolutionism is the religious
philosophy which governs the teaching of the
ideologies and moral structure of civilization in
the public school, then Christians had surely
better be about the business of installing
creationism as the basic philosophy of the
Christian school, unless they are willing to let our
entire civilization and its moral structure be
governed by the humanistic world view and all
the anti-Christian applications which that entails.

PRESSURES ON THE CHRISTIAN SCHOOL

Every Christian (and every concerned American
citizen, for that matter) needs to be constantly
aware, also, that the humanistic world view also
embraces world government and world religion.
These idealogues (whether of the Marxist left or
the Fascist right, whether atheists or pantheists)
will never be satisfied with controlling just the
public schools. They desire also to control all
private schools and *especially* Christian schools,
since they want to establish mind control of all
people everywhere. Many of these people may
have what they consider noble motives in this
goal (to free the world from war, from pollution,
from bigotry or whatever), but the bottom line is
that they want complete control of all education.

Eternal vigilance is the price of liberty, and
Christians need to be constantly alert to attempts
to gain ideological control of their Christian
schools by the humanists of the educational

establishment. There have already been numerous attempts by these secular educators and political manipulators to usurp such control, and some of the attempts have been vicious indeed. In some situations, various governmental agencies have tried to control Christian schools through centrally approved textbooks, teacher licensing, etc. In other situations, especially at the college level, such controls are increasingly being exerted by ostensibly private (but actually at least quasi-governmental) regional and/or professional accreditation bodies. While these may all protest that they do not try to specify the school's educational philosophy or the content of its curricula, the fact is that this is being done today and will undoubtedly increase in the future. That is the very nature of the educational beast, and those who are the most committed to their humanistic goals are the very ones who seek whenever possible to acquire positions of power in such agencies and organizations.

In the very nature of things, it seems wrong for a Christian individual or a Christian organization to be "unequally yoked" with unbelievers in associations which seek idealogical control over the beliefs and practices of their members (II Corinthians 6:14-17). Why should a Christian school allow a group of unbelieving educators, following a set of humanistic criteria structured around evolutionary presuppositions, dictate the nature and content of its programs?

On the other hand, Christians do acknowledge the divinely authorized responsibility of human governments to provide for the protection and safety of their citizens. There is thus no problem with Christian schools being required to meet reasonable codes of construction and operational

safety, as well as financial responsibility, honesty
in advertising and other such general regulations.
As long as the accrediting or licensing commission limits its regulations to this kind of thing,
there would be no problem. Furthermore, most
Christian schools should have no objection if
their graduates were required to pass standardized
examinations for the basic proficiencies
required of other graduates for citizenship
responsibilities.

It is only when such agencies want to dictate
faculty, curriculum and philosophy that Christian
schools have the right and responsibility to
refuse. According to the Scriptures, education is
the province of the home and church, not the
government, and certainly not that of some
humanistically oriented organization of
secular educators.

Many administrators of Christian schools and
colleges will argue, however, that the accrediting
and licensing agencies really don't try to evaluate
a school's philosophy and purpose but only its
effectiveness in doing what it professes to do.
This may be true in some cases, but it is certainly
not always true, and there is always the uncer-
tainty as to whether it will be true the next time
around, after it is too late to escape their control.

One should remember that whatever the
reason, most Christian colleges and seminaries
have, indeed, compromised their standards of
doctrine and conduct since their original founding, and this is especially true with respect to the
doctrine of creation. The pressures toward
accreditation and conformity are bound to have
played some part in this decline. Of course, "none
dare call it compromise." No one who compromises a doctrinal position ever seems willing

to admit, even to himself, that it was actually a compromise. There will always be rationalizations and self-justifications, and the accommodation will always be more apparent to knowledgeable outsiders than to those who are directly involved. One rule of thumb worth remembering is that, while one may be able to explain away a compromising position, a no-compromise position does not even *need* an explanation!

In any case, whatever may have been the situation in the past, there should be little doubt about the future. With the opposition to creationism and Christian fundamentalism growing more desperate and strident all the time, along with the implacable desire of the humanistic establishment to control education, Christians can be certain that pressures to compromise, especially on the doctrines of creation and Biblical inerrant authority, will increase.

THE PROPHETIC FUTURE

This tremendous age-long conflict between the two world views, evolutionary humanism and monotheistic creationism, should be of vital concern to every Christian, regardless of denomination, and certainly without regard to his or her particular point of view on Biblical prophecy. Bible-believing Christians of every shade of prophetic belief ought to be concerned about the real dangers involved in the rising tide of evolutionary humanism, which is threatening the very existence of Biblical Christianity in the "new age" of the immediate future.

Furthermore, whether the "last days" prophesied so often in the Bible are very near, already here, or yet sometime in the future, it is

certain that our own generation is nearer to the
last days than any generation before us. We
would do well, therefore, to heed what the
Scriptures tell us about the last days, especially
with reference to the imminent consummation of
the great conflict of the ages. Note, in particular,
four prophetic vignettes of the last days, as given
by four key human authors of the Holy Spirit-
inspired Scriptures.

PAUL AND HUMANISTIC EDUCATION

The Apostle Paul's most cogent prophecy of the
last days is found in his final book,
written shortly before his martyrdom, in II
Timothy 3:1-4:4. "In the last days perilous times
shall come," he said. Then follows a somber
recital of those attributes of the last days that
will make them "perilous times" (or, more literally,
fierce times). Every descriptive word or phrase in
the list could be applied specifically to one or
another form of humanistic philosophy, from the
first in the list — "lovers of their own selves" —
to the last — "ever learning, and never able to
come to the knowledge of the truth."

Humanists, of course, altogether reject divine
revelation and authority, maintaining that, while
people should search for truth, they can never
really find it, since there are no absolutes. It is
also pointed out by Paul that the philosophy
behind the behavior is a non-supernatural
religion — "having a form of godliness, but
denying the power thereof."

Finally, the fact that all these humanistic
beliefs and practices are especially focussed on
education, is stressed in the last verses of the
passage:

> "For the time will come when they will

> not endure sound doctrine; but after
> their own lusts shall they heap to
> themselves teachers, having itching
> ears; And they shall turn away their ears
> from the truth, and shall be turned unto
> fables."

Probably the most significant thing about this
list of characteristics of the false teachers of the
last days and their followers is its close similarity
to the list of characteristics of the pagans of the
primeval days, as given by Paul in Romans
1:28-32. That is, the humanism of the anti-
Christians of the last days will be essentially
identical with the pagan idolatary of the early
days.

And this humanistic, religious system of the
ancient days, now being revived in the latter
days, is based explicitly on the wilful denial of
creation and the Creator:

> "For the invisible things of Him from the
> creation of the world are clearly seen,
> being understood by the things that are
> made, even His eternal power and
> Godhead, so that they are without
> excuse: Because that, when they knew
> God, they glorified Him not as God,
> neither were thankful; but became vain
> in their imaginations, and their foolish
> heart was darkened. Professing
> themselves to be wise, they became
> fools, and changed the glory of the un-
> corruptible God into an image made like
> corruptible man, and to birds, and to
> four-footed beasts, and creeping things.
> Wherefore God also gave them up to
> uncleanness through the lusts of their
> own hearts, to dishonor their own bodies

between themselves,; who changed the
truth of God into a lie, and worshipped
and served the creature more than the
Creator, who is blessed for ever. Amen"
(Romans 1:20-25).

This system is nothing but evolutionism,
whether it takes on the outward form of
polytheistic idolatry or that of humanistic
naturalism. Ultimate reality is believed to be
centered in the creation (expecially in corruptible
man) rather than in the Creator. Such a rejection
of God as Creator is inexcusable, because even
the creation which they worship bears irrefutable
testimony to the power and nature of God.

The phrase "without excuse" is especially
significant. In the original, it is "without an
apologetic" — that is, "indefensible." The evolutionary humanist must base his faith not on
scientific evidence but on credulity, since there is
no real evidence, no apologetic, no defense, no
excuse for believing in evolution instead of
special creation.

Nevertheless, as the last days move on to their
climax, "evil men and seducers shall wax worse
and worse, deceiving and being deceived" (II
Timothy 3:13). The Apostle Paul says in another
of his epistles that this humanistic religion of
man-worship will finally reach the point where a
great world ruler will proclaim himself to be God,
even though actually he is the ultimate man of
sin and son of perdition (II Thessalonians 2:3, 4).

But the Apostle does not leave us merely with a
prophecy of the humanistic education,
humanistic religion and humanistic government
which will increasingly dominate the scene in the
last days. He also tells us, as the Christians of the

last days, what should be our response.

> "Continue thou in the things which thou
> hast learned. . . . The Holy Scriptures are
> able to make thee wise unto salvation,
> through faith which is in Christ Jesus. ...
> All Scripture is given by inspiration of
> God, and is profitable . . . that the man
> of God may be perfect. . . . Preach the
> word; be instant in season, out of
> season; reprove, rebuke, exhort with all
> long-suffering and doctrine" (II Timothy
> 3:15-4:2).

This is probably the greatest passage in the Bible on the divine inspiration and authority of Holy Scripture, and it occurs right in the middle of Paul's frightening description of the revival of ancient evolutionary paganism in the last days under the guise of modern evolutionary humanism. In the midst of a world in its final and greatest rebellion against its Creator, he says, you must simply continue to believe and obey and proclaim the authoritative Word of God!

PETER AND CHRISTIAN APOSTASY

Peter's great prophecy of the last days, like Paul's, occurs toward the end of his own final epistle to Christian believers. As will be discussed in Chapter VI, II Peter 3:3-6 is especially significant in a discussion of the Flood, but actually the entire third chapter of II Peter is of tremendous value to the discerning Christian of the last days.

Peter begins by stating his desire to "stir up your pure minds" — not just our pure emotions! The straight, clear, uncorrupted thinking of the "sound minds" which God has given (II Timothy 1:7) will be urgently needed in the last days.

Then comes Peter's description of the last-day
scoffing humanists, who reject God's promise of
His coming consummation of history in order to
"walk after their own lusts," rationalizing their
rebellion by denying there was ever a beginning
of history — that is, by denying creation. Peter
calls such a position one of "wilful ignorance"
(just as Paul had called it "indefensible"), in view
of the tremendous evidence for special creation
and the worldwide Flood.

But then Peter adds a special word of warning
to Christians. No only must they stir up their
minds with both Old and New Testament
teachings ("words spoken before by the holy
prophets," and "commandments of us the
apostles" - verse 2), but also they must specially
guard against the strong temptation to "wrest
the Scriptures" (verse 16) in hoping to
accommodate them to the evolutionistic
teachings of the last days.

The sad truth is that, in these latter days, there
have been multitudes of Christians and Christian
institutions that have done exactly that. They
have been so intimidated by the scoffing intellectual, arrogantly denying both the primeval
creation and the promised consummation, that
they have resorted to distorting the Scriptures,
trying somehow to justify accommodating the
system of evolutionary uniformitarianism in the
Biblical cosmogony. They have transmuted the
creation week into the geological "ages" and the
completed work of creation into an ongoing
process of "evolution." Wilfully in ignorance of
the worldwide Noahic cataclysm, they have made
Genesis teach a local flood, or a tranquil flood.
The fall of Adam through Satanic temptation
becomes merely the common experience of

everyone encountering the pull of his own lusts. Soon the Bible seems full of errors and Christ Himself becomes only an idealistic but somewhat misguided teacher.

Some such sequence of events as above outlined has been experienced by great numbers of churches, schools, missions, publications and other Christian institutions as they have "fallen from their own steadfastness' through a declension that began with "wresting the Scriptures" and ended with "their own destruction" (II Peter 3:16, 17). All of this, Peter predicted, would characterize "the last days." His antidote for such apostasy is the same as prescribed by Paul — "the Scriptures" — becoming "mindful of the words which were spoken before by the holy prophets, and of the commandment of us the apostles of the Lord and Savior" (verses 16, 2).

JOHN AND THE EVERLASTING GOSPEL

The Apostle John also has much to say about the last days. In fact, his final book — the Revelation — deals almost entirely with the prophetic future. There are many passages in Revelation which tie back in to Genesis, showing that all of God's purposes in creation will finally be accomplished at the consummation.

It is not surprising, therefore, that he sees the doctrine of primeval creation assuming critical importance as the consummation draws near. For example, Chapters 2 and 3 of Revelation consist of seven letters, written to seven churches, taken as representative of all churches of all times and places, giving such counsel and special instruction as would be needed by every church in similar circumstances. It is significant that a clear reference to the imminent return of Christ is incorporated in each of the last four of these epistles (Revelation 2:25; 3:3; 3:11; 3:20), indicating that churches of these types will be in existence when Christ comes again.

The last of these — the church of the Laodicians — is typical of the church that seems prosperous and self-satisfied, claiming to "have need of nothing," but which inwardly is "neither cold nor hot," blissfully unaware of its "wretched, miserable, poor, blind, naked" spiritual condition. A lukewarm church is not an apostate church, cold and dead. It is one with the appearance of orthodoxy and emotional zeal, with fine facilities and a large budget. But it is neither cold nor hot, a fence-straddling, middle-of-the-road, com- promising church. It is a church that is very much like many conservative, evangelical — even fundamental — churches in the world today.

Therefore, the way in which the Lord Jesus Christ begins His message to such churches is highly significant. "These things saith the Amen, the faithful and true witness, the beginning of the creation of God" (Revelation 3:14). Such a saluta- tion clearly points up the foundational importance of an uncompromising testimony, stressing especially the fact of creation and the identity of Christ as Creator. This apparently is the corrective that will be urgently needed by many outwardly orthodox and active churches in the last days.

In the next chapter of Revelation, John is translated to the heavenly throne, where he sees the twenty-four elders, representing all redeemed saints, praising the Lord for His great work of creation (Revelation 4:11). Since that will be the occupation of translated believers immediately after the second coming, it is obvious that it *should have been* their testimony just before the second coming.

Soon afterwards on the earth, amid scenes of great tribulation, an ominous development is seen by John. A great man, blaspheming the name of God and persecuting all Christians, acquires power over all other men and demands to be obeyed and worshipped as though he himself were God (Revelation 13:4-8, 15-18).

This is humanism come to full fruition, with men worshipping a representative man, the pinnacle of the supposed long evolutionary process leading upward to man and finally to superman, as God. Not only, however, will the world worship this "Beast;" but ungodly men and women throughout the world will finally come to realize that there really is a Creator God, and then they will consciously choose Satan instead of God, "worshiping the dragon which gave power unto the beast" (Revelation 13:4) and thus, as in primeval days, "worshiping and serving the creature more than the Creator, who is blessed for ever. Amen" (Romans 1:28).

It is in the context of this fearful climax of evolutionary humanism on earth that John then sees a unique evangelistic witness beginning to sound forth.

> "And I saw another angel fly in the midst of heaven having the everlasting gospel to preach unto them that dwell on the earth, and to every nation, and kindred, and tongue and people, Saying with a loud voice, Fear God, and give glory to Him: for the hour of His judgment is come: and worship Him that made heaven, and earth, and the sea, and the fountains of water" (Revelation 14:6, 7).

The *everlasting gospel* (thus the one true
gospel, which can never change) stresses in this
awful coming day, the urgent call to worship the
Creator! This Creator is, of course, the same Lord
Jesus who became Redeemer, and the gospel
includes acknowledgment of this truth also (I
Corinthians 15:1-4). But it is profoundly
important, especially as these dreadful final days
of humanistic world rule approach, to stress as
the angel will — the vital importance of recognizing and worshipping the Creator God as
Sovereign of all creation.

DAVID AND THE KING OF CREATION

One more prophetic vignette will be considered,
this time from the Old Testament. The psalmist,
King David, lived and wrote practically at the
mid-point of human history as recorded and fore-
seen in the Bible. He wrote most of the chapters
in the book of Psalms which, of course, includes
the middle chapters of the Bible (the central
chapter, and also the shortest chapter in the
Bible, is Psalm 117).

The first of the Messianic psalms — that is,
those psalms which deal with the coming of
Christ (either His first coming, or second coming,
or both) — is the second psalm. This psalm,
interestingly, is specifically mentioned in the New
Testament, both as to number and as to author
(Acts 4:25; 13:33).

Psalm 2 is in the form of a dramatic poem,
consisting of four stanzas, each with three verses.
In the first stanza, David is apparently the
speaker; in the second, the scene shifts from
earth to heaven, where God the Father speaks. It
is apparently the Son of God who then speaks in
Stanza 3, while the last three verses contain a

convicting exhortation and invitation which could
well emanate directly from the Holy Spirit.

As the psalm begins, it seems that David is
experiencing an amazing prophetic vision. He
sees a great convocation — or perhaps many
such convocations — in which kings and other
leaders of human thought and action have
assembled for the purpose of making a
momentous decision. Once and for all, they think,
they are going to get rid of God, in order to set
up their own world system, centered in man.

David, sensing the enormity and utter folly of
such a blasphemous proposal, cries out: "Why?"
He goes on to say (literally):

> "Why do the nations tumultuously
> assemble themselves together and their
> peoples contemplate such a foolish
> thing? The kings of the earth set
> themselves, and the rulers take counsel
> together, against Jehovah, and against
> His Christ, saying, Let us break their
> bands asunder, and cast off all their
> restraints from us" (Psalm 2:1-3).

World leaders — political, intellectual, financial
and other "rulers" — decide the time has finally
come to root out all the vestiges of the old
religions centered in a Creator God and His
Redeeming Son, replacing them with a religion of
their own, a religion no doubt centered in man
and his unrestrained lusts for power, affluence
and pleasure. Any such decision and action by
world leaders would, of course, establish a
religion of evolutionary pantheistic humanism,
and David cries out: "Why?"

This decision — now being foreshadowed in a
multitude of councils and conventions and all

kinds of meetings all over the world — will be a dreadful and fateful action for the world and its people, and will signal an awful wave of persecution for Christians. But the great Creator Himself will not be intimidated by such a declaration.

> "He that sitteth in the heavens shall laugh: the Lord shall have them in derision" (verse 4).

This is surely one of the most awesome and terrible verses in the Bible. To be the object of ridicule by the God who is love, the God of all grace, the only wise God, the almighty one, the God of all comfort, the heavenly Father, the eternal God, the God of hope — to be ridiculed and derided by such a God must be an inconceivably terrifying experience that will never cease to haunt those who go through it, as long as hell endures.

Yet that is exactly what is coming for those who persist in their wicked determination to make man a god and who, "professing themselves to be wise, became fools" (Romans 1:22). God will surely set His King upon His holy hill of Zion (verse 6).

> "Then shall He speak unto them in His wrath, and vex them in His sore displeasure" (verse 5).
> "Thou shalt break them with a rod of iron: thou shalt dash them in pieces like a potter's vessel" (verse 9).

With such a forbidding prospect looming ahead, these leaders of humanistic thought and policy would surely be well advised to heed the final warning of the Spirit:

> "Be wise *NOW* therefore, O ye kings: be
> instructed, ye judges of the earth. Serve
> the Lord with fear, and rejoice with
> trembling. Kiss the Son, lest He be angry
> and ye perish from the way, when His
> wrath is kindled but a little. Blessed are
> all they that put their trust in Him"
> (Psalm 2:10-12).

Thus, whatever the events of the years just ahead
may be, the ultimate outcome of the conflict is
not in doubt. It really does not matter if all the
world's political heads and the intellectual
leaders join in battle against the God of creation
and salvation. As David predicted three thousand
years ago, when he saw in vision this great future
rebellion of these "great ones" of the earth, their
ultimate end is complete defeat.

Over a thousand years later, John the Apostle
saw perhaps the same great end-time rebellion,
and again prophesied its destruction.

> "These shall make war with the Lamb,
> and the Lamb shall overcome them: for
> He is Lord of Lords, and King of kings:
> and they that are with Him are called,
> and chosen, and faithful"
> (Revelation 17:14).

Let all those who are tempted to compromise
with the leaders of the world system in *this* day
reflect that, in *that* day, it will be better to have
been with Him, than with them!

PART II

CREATION AND THE WITNESS OF TRUE SCIENCE

Chapter IV

Science Falsely So Called

THE TESTIMONY OF REAL SCIENCE

In this scientific age, one of the most effective tools for leading people to Christ ought to be the use of scientific Christian evidences. The very real scientific accuracy and insights of the Scriptures, the innumerable scientific evidences of creative design in nature, and the marvelous correlation of the Biblical world view with that evidenced by all the real facts of science, all could and should be effective in pointing the minds and hearts of people everywhere to both the Word of God and the God of the Word.

CHRISTIAN NEGLECT OF SCIENCE

The problem is that most Christians have, in effect, surrendered science to the unbelieving world. they have been told so often that "the Bible is not a book of science," and that it is somehow unspiritual to mix science with moral and religious concerns that they have usually tried to keep spiritual and scientific issues in separate mental compartments. Furthermore, they have been so indoctrinated, in school and by the news media, that the Bible contains many

scientific errors (especially on the questions of
creation and the flood and the age of the earth)
that, even though they don't really believe these
allegations, they are afraid they can't answer
them effectively, and so try to pass them off
as unimportant.

This defeatist attitude is unnecessary and is
itself unspiritual. All *truth* (and the very word
"science" means *knowledge*) is God's truth and
therefore, if rightly understood and applied, must
point men to Him. The very heavens declare His
glory and the invisible things of God, even His
eternal power and Godhead, are clearly seen in
the creation (Psalm 19:1; Romans 1:20).

By far the greatest obstacle to the effective use
of science in Christian witnessing is the
widespread and repeated propaganda to the
effect that evolutionary "science" yields the true
understanding of the world. A secondary excuse
used by many Christians is that science is too
specialized and complicated for them to understand and use in such a way. Neither assumption
is valid.

We have already shown, in Chapter II, that
evolution is not science at all, but religion — and
false and harmful religion at that. That the up-to-
date facts of true science support creation and
the Bible, while refuting evolution and humanism,
will be further documented in this chapter. There
is certainly nothing to fear, and everything to
gain, in applying genuine science to the study
and support of the Bible in all its aspects. These
facts can, indeed, be used effectively in Christian
evangelism, and this also can be firmly
documented.

As far as the specialized nature of science is
concerned, it is true that there is great need for

talented young Christian men and women to become professionals in the various fields of science, not simply to evangelize other scientists, but actually to bring the sciences themselves to Christ, organizing all the data and concepts of their respective fields within the Biblical framework of creation and redemption.

Nevertheless, the basic principles of the various sciences are set forth in the Scriptures and can easily be understood and used in witnessing by anyone who will make a little effort to learn them. In view of such commandments as I Peter 3:15 and II Timothy 2:15, every Christian can and should be willing to do this.

THE TRUE NATURE OF SCIENCE

Science once was recognized as the organized body of known truth, or at least as a *search* for truth. It dealt with *facts*, demonstrated facts. The essence of the scientific method was formerly considered to be experimentation and observation, involving factual predictions which could be tested and at least in principle, either falsified or confirmed by measurement. Evolution, of course, cannot be tested or falsified in its broad scope, and thus is not real science. However, if it is regarded as a scientific model, which is potentially true and can be evaluated as such in one's search for ultimate truth, then it is appropriate to include it in science classes on that basis.

It is interesting to note the definition of science in the first edition of Webster's Dictionary, published originally in 1828. In this venerable publication, the primary meaning of science is given as follows:

> In a general sense, knowledge, or certain knowledge, the comprehension or

understanding of truth or facts by the
mind. The science of God must be
perfect."

Current efforts to prevent the recognition of
"creation science" as appropriate for incorpora-
tion in science courses while still keeping evolution as the framework of such courses, however,
has led to redefining science essentially as
naturalism or even *materialism,* the attempt to
explain not only present-day processes and
systems in naturalistic terms, but even the *origin*
of all processes and systems in such terms. No
hint of supernatural origins can be allowed, even
though naturalistic explanations prove
completely inadequate to explain origins.

For example, entomologist Stanley Beck,
writing in the October 1983 issue of *Bioscience,*
all the while professing belief in
Christianity, says:

> Is scientific creationism scientific?
> Obviously it is not. Creationism involves
> a premise that lies outside of science. . .
> If separated from its origin in a religious
> tradition, might not the creationist view
> of life on earth be offered as a scientific
> theory? . . . The answer is an un-
> equivocal 'no,' because the creationist
> theory requires the belief that some
> force, some factor has created and, in so
> doing, has by-passed the natural forces
> and mechanisms by which the physical
> universe operates" (p. 270).

Thus God, who indeed is the true Creator of
heaven and earth, and who also created the very
forces and mechanisms which now operate His

created universe, is summarily refused any recognition at all, even by many who claim to believe in Him, by such arbitrary semantic circumlocutions. If scientists are really searching for truth, and not merely serving as promoters of atheistic humanism, they should at least allow the possibility that truth could include creation.

If Christians will simply keep these distinctions in mind, they need never be intimidated by naturalistic scientists or other skeptics. Whenever someone says that science has proved evolution, simply ask him to cite *and document* one scientific *proof* of evolution, reminding him that "science" means *knowledge*, not theory or assumption or speculation. There has never yet been presented one real scientific proof of evolution, or even any good evidence. The same applies to the supposed great antiquity of the earth and the universe.

Similarly, when anyone alleges that the Bible contains scientific mistakes, ask him to cite and document one of them. Once again, if he is honest, he will eventually have to back down.

On the other hand, there are numerous statements in the Bible which are scientifically accurate, as well as innumerable evidences of creation in nature. Many of the Biblical statements of scientific fact preceded their confirmation by scientists by thousands of years. Such facts can be cited and explained, both as evidence of creation and also as evidence of Biblical inspiration. Real science will always be found to support creation and the Bible.

A brief survey of some of these scientific evidences is given in this chapter, with current data and documentation. For those desiring further discussion of these important topics,

Appendix A gives a number of selected references which should be helpful.

THE BASIC LAWS OF SCIENCE

Among the most significant Biblical foreshadowings of modern science are the two most universal and best-proved principles of science. These two generalizations are, of course, the famous first and second laws of thermodynamics. They can actually be considered not only as scientific laws but as divine laws, laws which control the interactions of all components of every process known in every field of science.

THERMODYNAMICS IN THE BIBLE

The first law of thermodynamics is perhaps better known as the law of conservation of energy. It states simply that the total amount of energy (including mass, as well as light, heat, sound, electricity and all other forms of energy) in the universe is conserved. Energy can neither be created nor annihilated. This simple statement expresses the basic constraint that governs every process in the physical universe, so far as known. Since every thing and every phenomenon is essentially composed of one or more forms of energy, the first law of thermodynamics assures us that nothing is now being either created or destroyed.

This law was formally stated as a firm principle of science only a little more than a hundred years ago, but the truth which it formalizes is right at the end of the primeval creation account itself.

"Thus the heavens and the earth were finished, and all the host of them. And

> on the seventh day God ended His work
> which He had made; and He rested on
> the seventh day from all His work which
> He had made. And God blessed the seventh
> day, and sanctified it: Because that in it
> He had rested from all His work which God
> created and made" (Genesis 2:1-3).

That is, after God had finished creating and making everything in the universe into complete functioning, continuing systems, He "rested." He
stopped His work (= energy) of creating, and
instituted His ongoing principle of "conserving"
what He had created. He has, ever since, been
"upholding all things by the word of His power"
(Hebrews 1:3). To all intents and purposes, these
operations constitute what we now call the First
Law, the Law of Conservation.

The Second Law is also known as the principle
of increasing entropy, where "entropy" is a
mathematical term which measures the state of
disorganization in a system, or the energy which
(even though still in existence) can no longer per-
form useful work. This also is a universal law, ap-
plicable to all processes and systems, including
living organisms, with no known exceptions. It
can be stated in many different (but equivalent)
ways, depending upon the particular type of process involved. In all of them, however, it
describes a "downhill" tendency in nature.
Energy becomes less available, complexity breaks
down, structure becomes disarrayed, information
becomes confused — everything tends to deterior-
ate, if left to itself to do what comes naturally.

This also is a reflection of a primeval divine
pronouncement. "Cursed is the ground for thy
sake; . . . for dust thou art, and unto dust shalt

thou return" (Genesis 3:17-19). Because of man's sin, everything — even including the human body, which is the most complex system in the universe — is to be in a state of returning to the dust of the earth, the basic elements God had "created" in the beginning, and from which He had "made" all the intricate structures and systems of the cosmos. Since they had all been placed under man's "dominion," they were all brought under man's curse.

Thus the two most important, universal and best-proved laws of science, the first and second laws of thermodynamics, were enacted by God at the completion of His creation, and the pronouncement of His curse on the creation, respectively. They were then recorded in Scripture thousands of years before their recognition as scientific laws by modern scientists.

ENTROPY VERSUS EVOLUTION

Creationists have long emphasized the contradiction between evolution and the entropy law. The concept of evolution describes the universe as proceeding "uphill," from a primeval state of chaos to eventual perfection. Particles are believed to evolve into molecules, nonliving molecules into reproducing cells, simple organisms into complex organisms, apelike primates into human beings, and primitive cultures into utopia.

The principle of increasing entropy on the other hand, describes the scientific fact that the universe is now heading "downhill," from primeval order to eventual chaos. Stars and planets disintegrate, organisms die, species become extinct, materials wear out and order disintegrates into disorder. Although evolutionists have been reluctant to recognize the basic contradiction, they are increasingly acknowledging that the entropy law specifies the future of the world.

A recent bestselling book, for example, is entitled *Entropy: A New World View* (Viking Press, 1980). The author, Jeremy Rifkin, director of the Peoples' Business Commission and a radical social theorist, maintains that all the world's seemingly unsolvable problems (depleted resources, global pollution, escalating inflation, new diseases, runaway unemployment, bloated bureaucracies, etc.) are due basically to the law of increasing entropy.

All man's efforts toward progress and economic growth (in other words, attempting to reverse entropy) seem to require still more energy and therefore hasten the ultimate decay. The only hope, in Rifkin's view, is for the whole world to revert to a low-population, low-energy, very simple life-style.

The Bible, however, contains a better solution, both for the cause of this universal decay principle and for victory over it.

> "For the creation was made subject to vanity, not willingly, but by reason of him who hath subjected the same in hope. Because the creation itself also shall be delivered form the bondage of corruption into the glorious liberty of the children of God" (Romans 8:20, 21).

The popular syndicated columnist, Sydney Harris, recently commented on the evolution/entropy conflict as follows:

> "There is a factor called 'entropy' in physics, indicating that the whole

universe of matter is running down, and ultimately will reduce itself to uniform chaos. This follows from the Second Law of Thermodynamics, which seems about as basic and unquestionable to modern scientific minds as any truth can be.

At the same time that this is happening on the physical level of existence, something quite different seems to be happening on the biological level: structure and species are becoming more complex, more sophisticated, more organized, with higher degrees of performance and consciousness" (Field Enterprise Syndicate, as appearing in San Francisco *Examiner*, January 27, 1984).

As Harris points out, the law of increasing entropy is a universal law of *decreasing* complexity, whereas evolution is supposed to be a universal law of *increasing* complexity. Creationists have been pointing out this serious contradiction for years, and it is encouraging that at least some evolutionists (such as Rifkin and Harris) are beginning to be aware of it.

"How can the forces of biological development and the forces of physical degeneration be operating at cross purposes? It would take, of course, a far greater mind than mine even to attempt to penetrate this riddle. I can only pose the question because it seems to me the question most worth asking and working upon with all our intellectual and scientific resources" (*Ibid.*).

This, indeed, is a good question, and one for which evolutionists so far have no answer. Some have tried to imagine exceptions to the Second Law at some time or times in the past, which allowed evolution to proceed in spite of entropy, but such ideas are nothing but wishful thinking. Physicist Frank Greco says:

> "Being a generalization of experience, the second law could only be invalidated by an actual engine. In other words, the question, 'Can the second law of thermodynamics be circumvented?' is not well-worded and could be answered only if the model incorporated every feature of the real world. But an answer can readily be given to the question, 'Has the second law of thermodynamics been circumvented?' Not yet" (*American Laboratory Practice,* October 1982, p. 88).

Of course, the fact that no exception to the law of increasing entropy has ever been observed does not prove such a thing never happened. It simply shows that such ideas are outside the scope of science. Evolutionists are free to believe in such "singularities" by faith, if they wish (e.g., the inflationary universe, hopeful monsters, etc.) but they have no right to impose them on un-suspecting young minds in the name of science.

EVOLUTION AND OPEN SYSTEMS

The more common rejoinder to the apparent creation/evolution conflict, however, is simply to dismiss it as "irrelevant" on the basis of the naive and incorrect belief that entropy only increases in so-called "isolated systems" — that is, systems closed to any external organizing energy or information. Roger Lewin expresses this curious idea:

> "One problem biologists have faced is the apparent contradiction by evolution of the second law of thermodynamics. Systems should decay through time, giving less, not more, order.
>
> One legitimate response to this challenge is that life on earth is an open system with respect to energy and therefore the process of evolution sidesteps the law's demands for increasing disorder with time" (*Science,* September 24, 1982, p. 1239).

It is amazing how many anti-creationst debaters and writers try to "sidestep" this serious problem with such a simplistic cliche as this. Creationists who cite the entropy principle against the evolutionary philosophy are, time and again, dismissed as either ignorant of thermodynamics or dishonest in their use of the second law. Such charges are inappropriate, to say the least.

In the first place, the entropy principle applies at least as much to open systems as to closed systems. In an isolated real system, shut off from external energy, the entropy (or disorganization) will always increase. In an open system (such as the earth receiving an influx of heat energy from the sun), the entropy always *tends to increase* and, as a matter of fact, will *usually increase more rapidly* than if the system remained closed! An example would be a tornado sweeping through a decaying ghost town or a cast-iron wrecking ball imposed on an abandoned building.

Anyone familiar with the actual equations of heat flow will know that a simple influx of heat energy into a system *increases* the entropy of that system; it does not decrease it, as evolution would demand. Opening a system to external energy does not resolve the entropy problem at all, but rather makes it worse! The author of one of the most respected and widely used textbooks on thermodynamics, *Thermodynamics and Statistical Mechanics* (by Arnold Sommerfeld, Academic Press, 1956) says:

> "The statement in integral form, namely that the entropy in an isolated system cannot decrease, can be replaced by its corollary in differential form, which asserts that the quantity of entropy generated locally cannot be negative irrespective of whether the system is isolated or not, and irrespective of whether the process under consideration is irreversible or not" (p. 155).

Thus entropy (or disorganization) in an open system always at least tends to increase, no matter how much external energy may be available to it from the sun or any other source. If this tendency is to be overcome so that order in the system might be made to increase instead (as evolution would require), then the external energy must somehow be supplied to it, not as raw energy (like a bull in a china shop) but as organizing information. If the energy of the sun is going somehow to transform the nonliving molecules of the primeval soup into intricately complex, highly organized, replicating living cells, and then to evolve populations of simple organisms like worms into complex, thinking

human beings, then that raw energy has to be
converted into these evolutinary marvels through
some kind of unknown but very complex codes
and specifically designed mechanisms. If such
codes and mechanisms are not available on the
earth, (and no one yet has any evidence that any
such things exist at all) then the incoming heat
energy will simply disintegrate any organized
systems that might accidentally have shown
up there.

DISSIPATIVE STRUCTURES

Evolutionists have hardly even considered this
problem as yet, let alone solved it. There are, to
their credit, a few theorists who have at least
recognized the problem and offered certain
speculations as to possible directions in which to
search for a solution. The one man whose
speculations have received the most attention
(even acquiring for him a Nobel Prize in 1977) is
Belgian physicist Ilya Prigogine, who advanced
the strange idea of "dissipative structures" as a
possible source of new complexity in nature. He
postulated that when systems somehow are "per-
turbed" to a "far-from-equilibrium" condition, as
a result of a large influx of external energy which
produces an inordinate amount of internal energy
dissipation, then certain "structures" might be
generated. An example would be the generation
of storm cells in the earth's atmosphere by incoming solar heat.

How such "dissipative structures" could
possibly produce organic evolution is completely
unknown, and seems quite impossible to imagine.
Such systems in no way contradict the principle

of entropy but rather are illustrations of entropy working overtime! A Harvard scientist, John Ross, comments:

> ". . . there are no known violations of the second law of thermodynamics. Ordinarily the second law is stated for isolated systems, but the second law applies equally well to open systems. . . . there is somehow associated with the field of far-from equilibrium phenomena the notion that the second law of thermodynamics fails for such systems. It is important to make sure that this error does not perpetuate itself" (*Chemical and Engineering News*, July 7, 1980, p. 40).

Nevertheless, the bizarre notion of generating organization through chaos has achieved a remarkable following in recent years, not only among evolutionists anxious for a solution to the entropy problem, but also among radicals desiring a scientific justification for social revolutions, as discussed in Chapter II. For example, UNESCO scientist Ervin Laszlo, has said (as quoted by Wil Lepkowski):

> "What I see Prigogine doing is giving legitimization to the process of evolution — self-organization under conditions of change. . . . Its analogy to social systems and evolution should be very fruitful" (*Chemical and Engineering News*, April 16, 1979, p. 30).

Space precludes dicussion here of the many speculative applications that have been related to Prigogine's suggestion since he "gave legitimization to evolution," as Laszlo put it (thus admitting by inference that evolution was illegitimate until Prigogine came along with this unique remedy for entropy). Typical of these is a paper by two leading evolutionary biologists, Edward Wiley and Daniel Brooks, who speculate (without proof, either biological or mathematical) that evolution is inevitably produced in a world increasing in entropy, through the mechanism suggested by Prigogine (*Systematic Zoology*, Vol. 31, No. 1, 1982). However, evolutionist Roger Lewin, reviewing their paper, calls their speculations mere "heuristic formulations" and then cites Prigogine himself as being mystified by it.

" 'I see how you can do this with molecules,' he told Brooks, 'but I don't see how you can do it with species. I don't understand the extrapolation' " (Lewin, *op cit*, p. 1239).

And neither does anyone else! If science is to be based on fact and evidence, rather than metaphysical speculations, then entropy does not explain or support evolution at all. In fact, at least until someone can demonstrate some kind of naturalistic evolution-directing code and a pre-existing array of energy conversion mechanisms controlled by that code to generate increased organized complexity in nature, the entropy laws seem to make any significant "vertical" evolution quite impossible.

The marvelously complex universe is not left unexplained and mysterious by this conclusion, however. It was *created* by the omnipotent and omniscient King of Creation! If evolutionists prefer not to believe this truth, they can make that choice, but all the real facts of science — especially the fundamental and universal law of entropy — support it.

THE COMPLEXITY OF LIFE

Closely related to these implications from the laws of science as to the impossibility of evolution in general is the very high improbability of the chance generation of even the lowest and simplest form of life from non-living components. Another way of stating the entropy law is that systems tend to go toward a state of maximum probability. This means, of course, that they go towards disorder and randomness. A state of complex organization in a system performing specific functions is very "improbable," thus needing an explanation. A state of random scattering requires no particular explanation, since that is just the way things tend to become if left to themselves long enough.

LIFE AND THE LAWS OF PROBABILITY

One can therefore analyze complex systems in terms of statistics and the laws of probability, by calculating the probability of their natural occurrence by random processes. When this type of analysis is applied to a living system — even one at the lowest level that could be imagined for any kind of reproducing system — it quickly becomes apparent that the probability is far too low for it ever to have come into existence by any kind of random occurence.

This type of calculation is relatively easy and straightforward, but does require some knowledge of both biochemistry and mathematics, so may be a little difficult for the average non-scientist. Fortunately, a Christian may easily refer to the work of others in this field, since many scientists — both Christians and non-Christians — have now published convincing analyses of this sort. For example, a remarkable "conversion" has recently been experienced by the famous British astronomer Sir Fred Hoyle, the originator of the "steady-state theory" of the origin of the universe and an outspoken atheist for many years. Sir Fred and another atheist colleague, mathematical astronomer Chandra Wickramasinghe, have been reluctantly driven to the conclusion that life must have been created by a Higher Intelligence, since it is far too complex to have arisen by natural processes.

Hoyle has not only given up his steady-state theory but now also insists that the "big bang theory" is untenable. He and Dr. Wickramasinghe had recently calculated the odds against the chance formation of life on earth to be less than one chance out of $10^{40,000}$ (a number represented by "1" followed by 40,000 "zeros"). Hence they had concluded that life must have somehow evolved in outer space and been translated to the earth. This is the theme of their book *Evolution from Space* (New York, Simon and Schuster, 1981, 176 pp.), as also summarized in their article, "Where Microbes Boldly Went" (*New Scientist*, Vol. 91, 1981, pp. 412-415).

This probability is so small that Sir Fred compared it to the chance that "a tornado sweeping through a junkyard would assembly a Boeing 747 from the materials therein" ("Hoyle on Evolution," *Nature*, Vol. 294, Nov. 12, 1981, p. 105).

But that is not all. Hoyle and Wickramasinghe also then calculated the probability that life would ever arise spontaneously anywhere in a universe of 15 billion light-years radius and at least 10 billion years old. They found even *this* to be less than one chance out of

1,000,000,000,000,000,000,000,000,000,000!
In this book, Sir Fred specifically says:

> "The likelihood of the formation of life
> from inanimate matter is one to a
> number with 40,000 noughts after it. . . .
> It is big enough to bury Darwin and the
> whole theory of evolution. There was no
> primeval soup, neither on this planet nor
> on any other, and if the beginnings of
> life were not random, they must
> therefore have been the product of pur-
> poseful intelligence."

He makes another fascinating comparison,
using a figure long familiar to speculative
evolutionists.

> "No matter how large the environment
> one considers, life cannot have had a
> random beginning. Troops of monkeys
> thundering away at random on
> typewriter keys could not produce the
> works of Shakespeare, for the practical
> reason that the whole observable
> universe is not large enough to contain
> the necessary monkey hordes, the
> necessary typewriters, and certainly not
> the waste paper baskets required for the
> deposition of wrong attempts. The same
> is true for living materials" (p. 148).

Quite reluctantly, these two atheists were thus
driven to creationism as the only answer! Dr.
Wickramasinghe had been a Buddhist, and since
Buddhism is a religion based on atheism and
evolutionism he had felt quite comfortable in it.
Now, however, according to an interview in the
London Daily Express (Aug. 14, 1981), he says,

"From my earliest training as a scientist,
I was very strongly brainwashed to
believe that science cannot be consistent
with any kind of deliberate creation. That
notion has had to be painfully shed. At
the moment I can't find any rational
argument to knock down the view which
argues for conversion to God. . . . Now
we realize that the only logical answer to
life is creation."

Unfortunately, they have not come yet to
believe in the God of the Bible, but rather in sort
of a pantheistic Intelligence who somehow
created life spores in other parts of the universe
which were then caused to drift to earth to form
the seeds of life on earth. They are surely not
Bible-believing fundamentalist Christians.

Nevertheless, even this much of a concession to
creationism, coming from two such eminent and
world-famous scientists, so infuriated the evolutionary establishment that both Hoyle and
Wickramasinghe have since been practically
ostracized and even persecuted by many of their
erstwhile colleagues. Such is the objectivity of
evolutionary "science!"

THE WEAK RESPONSE OF EVOLUTIONISTS

Some evolutionists complain that, since Hoyle
and Wickramasinghe are astronomers and
mathematicians rather than biochemists, they
are unqualified to make judgments about the
origin of life. However, many who *are* evolutionist
biochemists have made similar calculations, with
similar results (not to mention all the creationist
scientists who have made such calculations). One
of these is Dr. Hubert P. Yockey. In an article

entitled "Self-Organization Origin of Life Scenarios and Information Theory," he says:

> "The calculations presented in this paper show that the origin of a rather accurate genetic code, not necessarily the modern one, is a *pons asinorum* which must be crossed over the abyss which separates crystallography, high polymer chemistry and physics from biology. The information content of amino acid sequences cannot increase until a genetic code with an adaptor function has appeared. Nothing which even vaguely resembles a code exists in the physico-chemical world. One must conclude that no valid scientific explanation of the origin of life exists at present" (*Journal of Theoretical Biology*, Vol. 91, 1981, p. 26).

For those unfamiliar with Latin, *pons asinorum* means "bridge of asses," a colorful metaphor for an exceedingly difficult bridge to negotiate. If the rest of the jargon in the quotation is troublesome, the last sentence is clear enough, and that's what counts!

But when this or similar probability arguments are used in creation/evolution debates (I can speak from personal experience here) the evolutionists' incredibly weak response is usually something like: "Yes, but every individual combination of factors has exactly the same probability; the one that specifies life is no more improbable than any other, so the argument from probability is meaningless."

Yockey's response to such a naive reply is kind but pointed and helpful:

"A practical man will not believe a scenario which appears to him to have a very small probability. . . . . If a tossed coin is observed to fall heads ten times consecutively, a practical man will believe it to be two-headed *without examining it,* even though the sequence of all heads is exactly as probable as any other sequence" (*Ibid.,* p. 27).

One can easily calculate that the number of possible sequences in a ten-sequence coin toss is 1024 (or 2^{10}), so the probability of a sequence of heads ten times in a row is one out of 1024. Even though no "practical" gambler would bet on a thousand-to-one shot, this probability is really a very high probability compared to the extremely low probability of a chance assemblage of chemical molecules into a meaningful and functioning genetic code of any kind whatever. As Hoyle has shown (along with many others) the universe is neither big enough nor old enough for it ever to have happened even once by chance. Life must have been specially created.

CONDITIONS IN THE PRIMEVAL SOUP

Apart from the question of complexity and probability, there would also have to be just the right environmental conditions for any imaginary simple life form to evolve from non-life and then survive and reproduce on the primitive earth. The speculations associated with this scenario — especially in view of the fact that the "spontaneous generation" of bacterial life in the present world was completely disproved by Louis Pasteur a hundred years ago — have been wildly imaginative, to say the least.

For more than 25 years, schoolchildren have been taught the imaginary drama of life's beginning on the primeval earth perhaps 3 billion years ago. The scenario has assumed an ancient atmosphere containing no oxygen, since an oxidizing environment would have destroyed any supposed molecules on the verge of evolving into living systems. Stanley Miller's famous laboratory apparatus by which he synthesized certain amino acids in a gaseous mixture simulating this hypothetical atmosphere has appeared on the pages of innumerable classroom textbooks, and the book *Origin of Life on Earth* by the Russian Communist Oparin, has been taught as dogma almost everywhere.

Now, however, like so many other evolutionary fables, the primeval "reducing" atmosphere is being dissipated by the hard facts of science. For more than a decade now, various scientists have been developing a wide range of evidences that the earth's atmosphere was rich in oxygen right from the beginning. In a recent study (*Geology*, Vol. 10, March 1982, pp. 141-146), two British geologists have accumulated a mass of geological evidence that the ancient earth never had a reducing atmosphere at all. They conclude:

> "The existence of early red beds, sea and groundwater sulphate, oxidized terrestrial and sea-floor weathering crusts, and the distribution of ferric iron in sedimentary rocks are geological observations and inferences compatible with the biological and planetary predictions. It is suggested that from the time of the earliest dated rocks at 3.7 b.y. ago, Earth had a oxygenic atmosphere"

(H. Clemmey and N. Badham, p. 141).

This fact means, of course, that life could never have evolved from non-life, at least by this method, and all the textbooks need to be re-written. But since belief in evolution is really religious rather than scientific, the scientists do not intend to become creationists. Rather, they merely search for another evolutionary scenario. The one they suggest currently is that life evolved somewhere else in the universe and was transported to earth!

EXTRA-TERRESTRIAL LIFE

Amazingly enough, many scientists are seroiusly proposing now that life evolved in outer space and then somehow reached the earth. As mentioned, Sir Fred Hoyle is one of these. Two other notable scientists, Sir Francis Crick (co-discoverer of DNA) and Leslie Orgel, of the University of California at San Diego, are promoting the curious notion of "directed panspermia" (life-sperms are everywhere in space and some have been directed by advanced galactic civilizations to the earth!), and this idea is receiving serious attention and wide acceptance. Both Orgel (*New Scientist,* April 15, 1982, pp. 149-152) and Crick (*Life Itself,* Simon and Schuster, 1981) have made calculations and strong statements about the impossibility of chance origin of life on earth. Crick says, for example:

> "If a particular amino acid sequence was selected by chance, how rare an event would this be? . . . Suppose the chain is about two hundred amino acids long; this is, if anything, rather less than the average length of proteins of all types.

> Since we have just twenty possibilities at
> each place, the number of possibilities is
> twenty multiplied by itself some two hun-
> dred times. This is approximately equal
> to . . . a one followed by 260 zeros. . . .
> The great majority of sequences can
> never have been synthesized at all, at
> any time" (p. 51).

Sir Francis then makes the following fascinating
admission:

> "An honest man, armed with all the
> knowledge available to us now, could
> only state that in some sense, the origin
> of life appears at the moment to be
> almost a miracle, so many are the condi-
> tions which would have had to have been
> satisified to get it going" (p. 88).

But since he believes neither in God nor
miracles, the eminent Dr. Crick opts for directed
panspermia. This is despite the fact that there is
not the slightest evidence anywhere (except in
science fiction and various occult religions) of
directed panspermia or anything else approximating extra-terrestrial human or animal life. The
entire notion brings us once again to the
threshold of an esoteric Marxism. As Yockey says:

> "Faith in the infallible and comprehen-
> sive doctrines of dialectic materialism
> plays a crucial role in origin of life
> scenarios, and especially in exobiology
> and its ultimate consequence, the doc-
> trine of advanced extra-terrestrial
> civilization. That life must exist
> somewhere in the solar system or
> 'suitable planets elsewhere' is widely and

tenaciously believed in spite of lack of
evidence, or even abundant evidence to
the contrary" (H.P. Yockey, *op cit*. p. 27).

The extraordinary weakness — in fact complete
absence — of any scientific evidence for a
naturalistic origin of life anywhere in the universe
is a well-kept secret of our establishment science,
education and news media. Christians need to
know this fact — and use this fact — in their
testimony to the world. It will be enlightening and
effective in many hearts.

The only true and scientific account of life's
origin is in the Bible. "He giveth to all life, and
breath and all things" (Acts 17:25).

THE MYSTERIOUS MECHANISM OF EVOLUTION

Evolutionists, in response to the creationist attack on evolution, repeatedly pledge allegiance
to evolution with the littany: "Although we may
disagree about the mechanism of evolution, we
all agree on the fact of evolution." The "we," of
course, means the scientific/education establishment. The majority of the American people,
according to a 1979 Gallup poll, do *not* believe in
evolution, in spite of the fact that they were
taught in school to believe in it and are bombarded
almost daily with authoritative pronouncements
from the news media assuring them of the factuality of evolution. There are now thousands of
scientists who have also repudiated evolution and
become creationists even though most of these,
like myself, were indoctrinated in evolution and
formerly believed in it.

If it were so obvious that evolution is a fact,
one would think it would be possible to describe
its mechanism. If not, at least there ought to be

available some kind of scientific proof of evolution. But the only real evidence seems to be the fact that most intellectuals believe in it. "The scientists can't be wrong," was the parting shot with which a certain pastor once concluded our discussion on the subject, thereby convincing me that it was time to move my church membership. If there really were any real scientific evidence for real evolution, one would suppose they would have presented it by now. Instead they argue about mechanisms, and try to explain the absence of evidence.

GAPS IN THE FOSSIL RECORD

One of the most embarrassing of the missing evidences is the complete absence of any genuine intermediate forms, containing transitional structures, in the supposed fossil record of the evolutionary "history" of life.

> "The missing link between man and the apes, whose absence has comforted religious fundamentalists since the days of Darwin, is merely the most glamorous of a whole hierarchy of phantom creatures. In the fossil record, missing links are the rule" ("Is Man a Subtle Accident?" *Newsweek*, November 3, 1980, p. 95).

So begins a feature article reporting a remarkable conference held in October 1980 at Chicago's Field Museum of Natural History of "160 of the world's top paleontologists, anatomists, evolutionary geneticists and developmental biologists." The conference centered around the growing repudiation of classic neo-Darwinism (gradual evolution through accumulation of beneficial random mutations by natural selection) in favor of so-called "punctuated equilibrium," the idea that "macroevolution" occurs in quantum leaps, leaving no intermediate fossils to mark the transitional stages.

Sensitive to the fact that creationist scientists have made great headway in recent years among the general population by citing these universal fossil gaps in support of the creation model of origins, participants in the symposium protested that they were not creationists and that "evolution is a fact," even though few could agree on how evolution happens or could point to any of the transitional stages that occur whenever it happens to happen!

In a leading journal, *Science*, one author noted that the meeting was probably "one of the most important conferences on evolutionary biology for more than 30 years" (Roger Lewin "Evolutionary Theory under Fire," November 21, 1980, p. 883). According to this official publication of the American Association for the Advancement of Science:

> "The central question of the Chicago conference was whether the mechanisms underlying microevolution can be extrapolated to explain the phenomena of macroevolution. At the risk of doing violence to the positions of some of the people at the meeting, the answer can be given as a clear, No."

Thus, there are no mechanisms to show real evolution in action, and no transitional fossils to show that it ever happened at all.

EVOLUTIONARY STASIS AND PUNCTUATED EQUILIBRIUM

One of the most noticeable aspects of the theory of evolution, therefore, is its own continuing evolution! One would think that after almost 150 years of intensive study of supposed evolutionary mechanisms, we should know by now how it works. But the fact is that evolution is no better understood now than it was in the days of Charles Darwin. Evolutionists protest (too much, methinks!) that they *know* evolution is true, but it must be embarrassing for them to have to admit repeatedly that they still don't understand its mechanism.

The latest idea is *stasis* — that is, stability, "standing still." Paleontologist Steven M. Stanley (John Hopkins University) says,

> "The (fossil) record now reveals that species typically survive for a hundred thousand generations, or even a million or more, without evolving much. We seem forced to conclude that most evolution takes place rapidly, when species come into being by the evolutionary divergence of small populations from parent species. After their origins, most species undergo little evolution before becoming extinct" (*The New Evolutionary Time-table: Fossils, Genes and the Origin of Species*, Basic Books, Inc., 1981, Preface).

Similarly, Harvard University geologist Stephen Jay Gould has said,

> "Thus, our model of 'punctuated equilibria' holds that evolution is con-

centrated in events of speciation and
that successful speciation is an infre-
quent event punctuating the stasis of
large populations that do not alter in
fundamental ways during the millions of
years that they endure" ("Is a New and
General Theory of Evolution Emerging?"
Paleobiology, Vol. 6, No. 1, 1980, p. 125).

This is certainly fascinating. *Evolution,* which
means "change," is characterized mainly by
stasis, which means "no change"! The punctua-
tions which produce new species occur so rapidly
and so rarely that they can never be observed.
Since we can never observe evolution in action, it
is supposed to happen very rapidly when we are
not looking. No wonder it has been so hard to
learn how evolution works!

WHERE'S THE FOSSIL EVIDENCE?

For many years, evolutionists pointed to the
fossil evidence as the main "proof" of evolution,
citing it as the actual historical record of the
course of evolution over the supposed vast spans
of geologic time. More recently, however, the
debates, seminars and literature of the Institute
for Creation Research and other creationists have
made it widely known that there are literally no
true intermediate transitional forms in all the
billions of documented fossils. Even evolutionists
now acknowledge this, and the strange new
theory of "punctuated equilibrium" and "hopeful
monsters" has been replacing traditional
Darwinism as the generally accepted modern view
of evolution.

Thus the fossil evidence has fallen on hard
times. Now we find evolutionists claiming that

this is not the real evidence for evolution anyhow!

> "In any case, no real evolutionist, whether gradualist or punctuationist, uses the fossil record as evidence in favor of the theory of evolution as opposed to special creation" (Mark Ridley, "Who Doubts Evolution?" *New Scientist,* June 25, 1981, p. 831).

With the fossil "proof" repudiated, there is no longer any evidence for evolution that involves the time dimension and which, therefore, can be anything other than circumstantial. Within the few millennia of human observation, no one has ever observed a single case of real evolution, so all "evidences" must be based on inferences from similarities. Professor Ridley, who is in the Department of Zoology at Oxford University, stated that there are just three kinds of real evidence left for evolution.

> "The three arguments are from the observed evolution of species, from biogeography, and from the hierarchical structure of taxonomy" (*Ibid.*).

But these are no proofs at all! The fact that new varieties, or even "species," can be formed by selection of variants is accepted by all creationists as a provision of the Creator, to enable the created "kinds" to adapt to different environments without becoming extinct. The observed geographical changes in the specific charactertistics of plants and animals merely illustrate this divine provision. New varieties of moths or finches may arise in such a way, but no new *kind* can ever arise, as far as all evidence has ever shown.

As far as the "hierarchical structure" of taxonomy is concerned, (that is, the orderly arrangement of organisms into species, genera, etc.), Ridley himself admits that "it is possible to classify any set of objects into a hierarchy," so that the taxonomic classification system "is not an argument for evolution." However, he thinks that "if all species had been created separately, there is no reason why they should have been created with the same genetic code" (*Ibid.,* p. 833).

The creationist is amazed at such a statement! He would simply answer "Why not?" The genetic code is incredibly complex and beautifully efficient. It could never have arisen by chance, as already shown. It gives clear evidence of profound creative forethought and planning.

Now, *these* are the "proofs" of evolution! No wonder so many people are turning back to creationism today.

As far as other "similarities" are concerned — whether in comparative anatomy, comparative embryology, comparative physiology, comparative biochemistry, or any others — it should be obvious that these are better evidence for creation by a common Designer than descent from a common ancestor. In fact this entire type of study was originally developed by creationists, especially Linnaeus, who regarded it as, in effect, "thinking God's thoughts after him." Dr. Colin Patterson has recently reminded his fellow evolutionists of this important fact:

> "Linnaeus and his successors recognized genera, families and other categories on the basis of similarities in structure, and believed that each group had a set of

features which were its essence, or ideal plan, corresponding to something in the mind of the Creator. Comparative anatomy developed as a means of searching out these ideal plans" ("Cladistics and Classification," *New Scientist,* March 25, 1982, p. 303).

Patterson is Head of Paleontology at the British Museum of Natural History. The relatively new science of cladistics, which was the subject of his article, is a quantitative attempt to classify organisms without reference to their presumed evolutionary history, simply by means of similarities. It is proving highly effective, but has attracted scathing criticism from many doctrinaire evolutionists.

THE EVIDENCE FROM DEFECTS

Evolutionary reasoning is now taking even stranger turns. The ingenious Marxist evolutionist, Harvard's Stephen Jay Gould, has finally discovered a scientific "proof" of evolution.

For a hundred years and more, the remarkable adaptations of organisms to their environment have been considered as strong indicators of the efficiency of "natural selection." The supposed selection of favorable variations proved by random beneficial mutations is the essence of Darwinism, and especially neo-Darwinism, and has long been accepted by most evolutionists as the basic mechanism through which new species evolve. In fact, the reason for Darwin's success in the first place was that his theory seemed to provide a mechanism for explaining away the apparent evidences of design in nature. The remarkable relations of plants and animals to each other and to their environments has often been presented in glowing language as proof of the marvelous efficiency of natural selection. Actually, as many recent evolutionists have admitted, the very concept of natural selection as an agent of "evolution" is a tautology. Those organisms that "survive" are assumed to have been the "fittest" by that fact.

Creationists, of course, have always argued that, while natural selection is a real process that serves to eliminate unfit organisms, it could never create the complex, wonderfully adapted organisms found in the living world. Stephen Jay Gould has recently acknowledged that even William Paley, the great Christian advocate of design and "natural theology," taught *this* type of natural selection over half a century before Darwin (*Science*, April 23, 1982, p. 386). Creationists have argued persuasively that complex adaptations are evidence of creative design, not chance variations, and Gould has even admitted this. The British scientist Jeremy Cherfas has recently echoed Gould's thesis:

> "In fact, as Darwin recognized, a perfect Creator could manufacture perfect adaptations. Everything would fit because everything was designed to fit" (*New Scientist*, May 17, 1984, p. 29).

This admission, however, does not mean at all that Gould or Cherfas or their fellow evolutionists have decided actually to believe in creative design. They have simply decided that adaptations don't prove evolution after all.

> "It is in the imperfect adaptations that natural selection is revealed, because it is those imperfections that show us that

> structure has a history. If there were no
> imperfections, there would be no
> evidence of history, and therefore
> nothing to favor evolution by natural
> selection over creation" (*Ibid.*).

This is an amazing admission. The main
evidence against creation and for evolution is
that natural selection doesn't work! If there were
no "imperfect" structures in nature, the evidence
would all favor creation. No wonder evolution has
to be imposed by authority and bombast, rather
than reason, if this is its only real evidence!

As a matter of fact, this argument from
imperfections is merely a new wrinkle on the old,
discredited argument from vestigial organs.
These are structures that were believed to have
atrophied from once-useful structures to useless
vestiges. As S.R. Scadding, of the Zoology Department at Guelph University, comments:

> "Haeckel makes clear why this line of
> argument was of such importance to early
> evolutionary biologists. . . . It seemed
> difficult to explain functionless struc-
> tures on the basis of special creation
> without imputing some lack of skill in
> design to the Creator" (*Evolutionary
> Theory*, May 1981, p. 174).

Actually there are probably no real vestigial
organs and probably no imperfect adaptations in
nature. Scadding points out that the former list
of nearly 100 such organs in humans has now
dwindled almost to nothing (*Ibid.*, p. 175). The
same could be shown for most of Gould's alleged
"imperfections." But even if there really are any
vestiges or imperfections, this would be evidence
for degeneration, not evolution. Furthermore, as

Scadding notes, this type of "argument is a theological rather than a scientific argument, since it is based on the supposed nature of the Creator" (p. 174). In fact, a sound theological argument would recognize that there will indeed be some imperfections in the world, because there is sin in the world, causing "the whole creation" to travail in pain (Romans 5:12; 8:20-22).

Thus current arguments that point to nature's imperfections as evidence for evolution are not sound arguments either scientifically or theologically, and Christians should not be intimidated by them.

THE "SCIENCE" OF MAN'S ORIGIN

Physical anthropology (or paleoanthropology) is a relatively new field of science which claims to be able to discover the evolutionary development of *Homo sapiens* from unknown non-human ancestors. Its data are the fossils and artifacts of ancient humans and their supposed ape-like ancestors.

THE SCARCITY OF DATA

Actually the data are pitifully few, far too sparse to support a theory of human evolution. Since there must have been uncounted billions of these ancient people and their hominid ancestors during the supposed million years or more of their history, and since they are supposed to be the most recent (and therefore presumably best preserved) arrivals in evolutionary history, one would think there would be an abundance of transitional fossils for these anthropologists to study. Actually, there are none!

There are some fossilized bones and teeth, all

right, but the sum total of all the known fossils
that can be stretched in any way to appear as
somehow transitional between apes and men, or
as between anything else and men, would not fill
a coffin box (*Science Digest,* May 1982, p. 44).
Even those that have been found lend themselves
to all kinds of conflicting interpretations, and
there are almost as many different human
evolutionary family trees as there are
anthropologists to think them up. In fact, it
has been frequently noted that there are at least
as many anthropologists as there are fossil
specimens for them to study (*Ibid.*). Malcolm
Muggeridge, the noted British writer, has record-
the amazing nugget of information that 500 or
more doctoral theses were written on the subject
of the bones of the Piltdown Man, bones eventually
discovered to be a hoax (*The End of Christendom,*
Eerdmans Publ. Co., 1980, p. 59). One may be
pardoned for suspecting that anthropology, the
science of man, may be an easy field in which to
acquire a doctorate, but a hard way to earn a
living!

At the 1984 annual meeting of the American
Association for the Advancement of Science,
anthropologists came from all over the world to
New York City, to examine together the well-
publicized exhibit of all these fossils that had
been organized by the American Museum of
Natural History for a special showing, and then to
discuss the meaning of all of it. The meeting was
reported in a science journal as follows:

> "One sometimes wonders whether
> orangutans, chimps and gorillas ever sit
> around the tree, contemplating which is
> the closest relative of man. (And would

they want to be?) Maybe they even
chuckle at human scientists' machina-
tions as they race to draw the definitive
map of evolution on earth. If placed on
top of one another, all these competing
versions of our evolutionary highways
would make the Los Angeles freeway
system look like Country Road 41 in
Elkhart, Indiana" (*Science News,* Vol.
125, June 9, 1984, p. 361).

The fact is, there is no non-circumstantial
evidence whatever of human evolutionary
"ascent" from anything but other humans. There
may be fossil evidence of certain extinct apes and
certain extinct tribes of people, but there are no
real ape-men or other evolutionary intermediates.
Certain suggested circumstantial evidences (e.g.,
similarities) are not real evidence, since they are
explainable by creation at least as well as by
evolution. This whole spectacle is simply the product of the wishful thinking of evolutionary
humanists, who are determined at all costs to
destroy the straightforward, realistic, satisfying
and *true* Biblical record of the origin of the
human race.

THE AUSTRALOPITHECINES

When I was in school, I was taught that the
three conclusive proofs of human evolution were
Piltdown man, Peking man and Java man. These
famous discoveries, however, are no longer taken
seriously. Piltdown man was a hoax, Peking man
has been lost for forty years and Java man was
later admitted by its discoverer to be an artificial
construct of a human thighbone and the skull of
a gibbon. Other former "stars" in the ape-man

extravaganza were Nebraska man (an extinct pig) and Neanderthal man (now universally acknowledged to be modern man).

The current "star" in this long-running show is a supposed hominid (ape-man) named *Australopithecus* (meaning "ape of the south"), associated with a varied collection of fossil evidence, including Louis Leakey's Zinjanthropus, Richard Leakey's Skull 1470 and Carl Johanson's Lucy, as well as Mary Leakey's Laetoli fossil footprints. Although there has been sharp disagreement between Johanson and the Leakeys as to their exact role in evolution, they all now claim that these so-called "australopithecines" walked erect, like men, even though they had ape-like brains and skulls.

Nevertheless, the evidence against this view is growing. Dr. Yoel Rak describes the significance of the first discovered australopithecine ear bone.

> "It is substantially different from that of a modern man, and the dissimilarity exceeds that between the ear bones of *Homo sapiens* and the African apes. The new incus ("anvil") is of interest particularly in view of the unique advantages that ear ossicles (bones) have for taxonomic and phylogenetic (evolutionary) studies. The only other fossil hominid ear ossicles are from Iatseh and are indistinguishable from those of modern man" ("Ear Ossicle of Australopithecus Robustus," *Nature*, Vol. 279, May 3, 1975, p. 62).

Dr. Charles Oxnard, who has made the most extensive and careful studies of all anatomists on the australopithecine fossils, has said: "The fossil fragments are usually uniquely different from any living form; . . . they are as often as not reminiscent of the orangutan" (*American Biology Teacher*, Vol. 41, May 5, 1979, p. 273). He also argued strongly that these creatures could not have been erect walkers at all (*Ibid.*).

That the australopithecines were simply apes of some kind is evident also from their skulls, which have long been recognized as having the brain capacity (about 500 cubic centimeters) of a true ape. It was long believed, however, that their brains were at least probably human-like in shape. This now also turns out to have been quite wrong.

> "I expected the australopithecine natural endocasts to appear like miniature replicas of human brains because that had been the prevalent view in the scientific literature since 1925. . . . My analysis of the seven known australopithecine endocasts shows Radinsky's hunch was right: all of the convolutions that they preserve were apelike." (Dean Falk, "The Petrified Brain," *Natural History*, Vol. 93, September, 1984, p. 38.)

As far as the supposed Australopithecus footprints are concerned, they have no connection with the other fossils and are probably true human footprints: "The uneroded footprints show a total morphological pattern like that seen in modern humans . . . strikingly human in pattern" (*Science*, Vol. 208, April 11, 1980, p. 175). 1980, p. 175).

We are well justified in concluding that Australopithecus, whatever it was, had *no* genetic relationship to man.

THE ENIGMA OF HOMO ERECTUS

There is another group of fragmentary fossils collectively known as *Homo erectus*, believed by many paleoanthropologists to be intermediate between *Australopithecus* and *Homo sapiens*. Peking man and Java man, once believed to be in this group, are now mostly ignored. However, other fossils of *Homo erectus* have since been found in both Asia and Africa, and possibly even in Australia. These have been so identified mostly by their brain capacities, usually in the 700-800 cu. cm. range.

This factor alone, however, does not prove anything, since a considerable number of fully normal modern human beings are known to have skull capacities in this range. Furthermore, many modern people have heavy brow ridges and low sloping forheads, so these features don't mean too much either. One problem has been that the apparent ages of *Homo erectus* remains have often overlapped the dates assigned to *Australopithecus*, so that the two families are known now to have been living contemporaneously and even in the same geographical areas.

There is no doubt that *Homo erectus* ("erect man") had an upright posture. That he was truly human, rather than an erect ape, has recently been confirmed by studies of the brain endocast from the skull known as "1470," discovered a number of years ago by Richard Leakey.

> "An endocast from the Kenya National Museum, a *Homo habilis* specimen known as ER 1470, reproduces a human-like frontal lobe, including what appears

> to be Broca's area" (Dean Falk, *op cit*,
> p. 38.)

Since this part of the brain (Broca's area) is
known to control speech and is uniquely human,
it seems clear that at least this particular *Homo
erectus* specimen was a true man, even though
his cranial capacity was just over 750 cu. cm.

> "If we wish to identify one prime mover
> of human brain evolution, the endocast
> from ER 1470, with its human-like frontal
> lobes that contain what appears to be
> Broca's speech area in the left
> hemisphere, confirms what is suggested
> by comparing the behavior of apes and
> humans: it is language." (*Ibid.*, p. 39.)

The fact that *Homo erectus* was a true man,
rather than an ape-human intermediate of some
kind, has been further confirmed by the discovery
in late 1984 of the most complete *Homo erectus*
skeleton found to date, a boy estimated to be 12
years old, excavated in Kenya and believed by
evolutionists to have lived about 1.6 million years
ago, as based on radiometric dating of the ash
deposits in which it was found by anthropologists
Richard Leakey and Alan Walker.

> "The new find reveals that these ancient
> people had bodies virtually in-
> distinguishable from our own . . The
> skeleton showed that the boy stood 5
> feet 6 inches, taller than many of today's
> 12-year olds." (Boyce Rensberger,
> "Human Fossil is Unearthed,"
> *Washington Post*, October 19,
> 1984, p. A1.)

Except for the brain size (between 700 and 800

cu. cm.) the skull and jaw-bone looked "much like a Neanderthal" (*Ibid.*). Neanderthal man, of course, is now acknowledged by all evolutionary anthropologists to be true man, *Homo sapiens*. Thus, while *Australopithecus* is simply an ape of some kind, it is probable that *Homo erectus* is a true man, much like the extinct Neanderthal tribe. Quite possibly, fossils have been identified as *Homo erectus*, rather than *Homo sapiens*, simply because they happened to be members of the human race whose brain sizes were at the low end of the normal spectrum of brain-size variation, but otherwise they were probably normal human beings.

EVOLUTION OF APES FROM MEN?

If evolution were true, then the various stages of human evolution ought to be the best documented of all, since man is supposedly the most recent evolutionary arrival and since more people are searching for fossil evidence in this field than in any other. Nevertheless, as noted above, the actual evidence is still extremely fragmentary and very doubtful. Exactly which hominid fossils might be ancestors of man, as well as when and in what order, are still matters of heated dispute even among evolutionary anthropologists.

But that is not all. The long-sought common ancestor of man and the apes, especially of "Lucy" and the other "australopithecines", now seems to have turned up still living — at least according to a strange theory currently being promoted by a number of anthropologists. This is the pygmy chimpanzee, the "bonobo," an inhabitant of the Zaire jungles, which is "almost identical in body size, in stature and in brain size" to Lucy, supposedly the oldest fossil hominid (*Science News*, February 5, 1983, p. 89). The few differences are exactly what many think would characterize the common ancestor of the australopithecines as well as man and the modern apes. Such leading anthropologists as Vincent Sarich (University of California at Berkeley), Adrienne Zihlman (University of California at Santa Cruz) and Douglas Cramer (New York University) "have become the champions of the bonobo model, and they have based their claims primarily on studies of the anatomy of living apes and fossilized hominids" (*Ibid.*).

This is amazing. The pygmy chimpanzee progressively evolved into Lucy, Java Man, Neanderthal Man and modern man on the one hand, while evolving by various unknown routes into chimpanzees, orangs, gorillas and pigmy champanzees(!) on the other hand. This is the remarkable scenario currently being promoted.

However, these imaginary sequences run into further trouble when attempts are made to place them in chronological order, for the dates rarely agree with the assumed sequences. As a matter of fact, the data are so uncertain that some scientists are now seriously proposing that chimpanzees evolved from men. That is, apes have man-like ancestors instead of men having ape-like ancestors! Two British scientists have recently concluded: "We think that the chimp is descended from man, that the common ancestor of the two was much more man-like than ape-like" (*New Scientist*, September 3, 1981, p. 594).

Now, of course, there are no true intermediates anyhow, so neither ape nor man is really descended from the other. As the scientists (John Gribbin and Jeremy Cherfas) point out: "The problem, for the paleontologists, is that they lack the evidence to decide" (*Ibid.*, p. 592). Evolutionary paleoanthropology is a wonderland where one can be his own ancestor and no one knows which way is really up.

CHRONOLOGICAL CONFUSION IN HUMAN "EVOLUTION"

The gross uncertainties in the hoped-for relationships between apes and men and the extinct hominoids seem to be compounded with every new fossil discovery. One not-too-well known fossil is the so-called Petralona Man, *Archanthropus europaeus petraloniensis,* discovered some years ago in a Greek cave and the object of considerable study by Greek anthropologist Aris N. Poulianos. Dr. Poulianos has insisted, on the basis of detailed analyses, that Petralona man "died more than 700,000 years ago and is the most ancient European yet known" (*Current Anthroplogy,* Vol. 22, p. 287).

This would seem to make it a very important "missing link," but the australopithecine discoveries in Africa, whose dates apparently overlap with both *Home erectus* and *Archanthropus,* have received far more attention. One problem is the modern appearance of the latter.

> "The dating of the skull and its classification have been contentious for several reasons. The calcite-embedded cranium was never photographed before its removal and there is considerable uncertainty about the sequence of sedimentary events in the cave. Then, anatomically, the skull presents a confusing mixture of primitive and modern

features, some characteristic of *Homo erectus* and some that could be ascribed to early *Homo sapiens"* (*New Scientist* Vol. 91, August 13, 1981, p. 405).

The human appearance of the skull is understated in most of the limited technical literature on this discovery, and the fact that the calcite in which it was originally embedded was a stalagmite is generally ignored altogether. For this kind of information, one must go to news accounts of the discovery, and to the first-hand reports of Dr. Poulianos:

> "The skeleton was found preserved in a stalagmite during an exploration of the Petralona Cave in the Chalkidiki Peninsula in southern Greece, said Dr. Aris Poulianos, President of the Greek Anthropological Society, Friday" (*Chicago Tribune,* June 6, 1976, in a Reuters dispatch from Europe).

Stalagmites, of course, are supposed to form extremely slowly, by the evaporation of water dripping from a cave roof. It would be impossible for fossils to be embedded and preserved under such conditions, so this is strong evidence that stalagmites can be formed quite rapidly under the right circumstances.

The fully human status of Petralona Man is further indicated by the following:

> "The discovery proves that the cave, which also contained primitive tools and cooked food, was inhabited by ape-age men who made intelligent use of fire. 'We discovered the cooked meat of rhinoceros, bear and deer, which proves

men who lived in the cave made logical use of fire,' Poulianos said" (*Ibid.*).

These discoveries, along with many evidences from other parts of the world, show that modern man lived at the same time as *Australopithecus, Homo erectus,* and other such supposed ancestors. Whatever these latter extinct creatures may have been, they could not have been ancestors of man.

There is another very "fuzzy" line of evidence that is being used by some evolutionists to try to work out supposed dates for the evolutionary separation of the various apes from the family tree culminating in *Homo sapiens,* or modern man. This is the so-called "molecular clock," which points to similarities in DNA, blood proteins, cytochrome C, and other biochemical factors as indicators of degree of relationship between creatures. The clock aspect is especially tied to the assumption that DNA mutation rates are constant with time, so that degrees of dissimilarity in DNA sequences can supposedly measure the recency of the date of evolutionary separation.

There is no need to discuss the technicalities of this subject here. The fact that it does *not* work should be settled by the results of extensive recent statistical studies. Alan Templeton, in the official journal of the Society for the Study of Evolution, has concluded:

> "Hence, for the gorilla-chimp-human portion of the phylogeny, there is a strong rejection of the molecular clock hypothesis. . . . Moreover, the molecular clock hypothesis was rejected at the 1% level" (*Evolution,* Vol. 37, March 1983,

pp. 238, 242).

This means, in effect, that there is 99% certainty that the molecular clock is meaningless as far as ape-human evolutionary chronology is concerned.

Templeton also comments on the general anthropological confusion as to the evolutionary relationships between various primates, as already discussed. He says:

> "Recent studies on hominid bipedalism and comparative studies with the other apes support the idea that bipedalism may have preceded the Hominidae and that a knuckle-walker, or even a brachiator, is a very poor model for a hominid ancestor. Therefore, these studies imply that humans did not evolve from knuckle-walking ancestors; rather knuckle-walking is far more likely to have evolved from partial bipedality" (Ibid., p. 241).

According to these studies, these "hominid" ancestors of man could walk on two feet ("bipedalism") before they evolved into either knuckle-walkers or brachiators (tree-swingers).

In concluding our discussion of this very mixed-up subject, we simply stress again that there is not one iota of real evidence for human evolution. All the tragic effects of this false assumption in human society, as summarized in Chapter II, were based flatly on the humanistic speculations of this strange fringe science called paleoanthropology ("the study of ancient man and his ape-like ancestors"). Christians should vigorously repudiate all such evolutionary speculations. Man has always been man since the very day he was directly created by God.

Chapter V

The Heavens and The Earth

ASTRONOMY AND THE BIBLE

The science of astronomy is one of the most ancient sciences, and the study of the glorious heavens has long been a testimony to the majesty and power of the Creator. The psalmist David proclaimed that "the heavens declare the glory of God" (Psalm 19:1) and the study of the stars led the wise men to seek the newborn Savior in Bethlehem. The father of modern astronomy, Johann Kepler, testified that in seeking to understand the planetary movements, he was merely trying to "think God's thoughts after Him," and the Christian astronomer William Herschel is said to have exclaimed that "the undevout astronomer is mad." The Bible's many passages dealing with the stars reveal a surprisingly modern perspective on stellar phenomena.

Yet the stars have somehow led others into deep apostasy. Astrology seems to head the list of the occult sciences, ancient and modern, and pagan idolatry has always centered in the worship of the host of heaven, often in the form of gross immorality and violent cruelty. In the modern era, the philosophy of naturalistic evolutionary humanism has permeated astronomy even more than biology. The astronomer Carl Sagan, with his impressive (but deceptively misleading) *Cosmos* television series, is perhaps the most visible and influential of our modern atheistic astronomers, but he is merely representative of most of the others. And before Sagan, there was Harvard's Harlow Shapley, who sought to replace "In the beginning, God" with "In the beginning, hydrogen," and capitvated the minds of multitudes with his popular series of Harvard books on astronomy. And then there were Fred Hoyle, of the steady-state theory, and George Gamow, of the big bang theory, with all their followers, all trying to explain the universe without God. But this is not possible.

THEIR HOST BY NUMBER

The study of the heavens certainly *ought* to bring men and women to acknowledge the Creator and His marvelous creation. As the prophet Isaiah said long ago: "Lift up your eyes on high, and behold who hath created these things, that bringeth out their host by number: He calleth them all by names by the greatness of His might, for that He is strong in power; not one faileth" (Isaiah 40:26). In such verses, the Christian has God's assurance that the proper study of astronomy and cosmology will build faith — not destroy it. But it does need to be approached from the Biblical point of view, not from an attempt to accommodate the false theories of humanistic astronomers.

"I will multiply thy seed as the stars of the heaven, and as the sand which is upon the sea shore" (Genesis 22:17), said God to Abraham, 4000 years ago.

Comparing the number of stars to the number of sand grains at first seems to be a very inappropriate simile. In Bible times, before the invention of the telescope, one could only see about 4000 stars. The Scriptures say that "the host of heaven cannot be numbered" (Jeremiah 33:22), but one could count up to 4000 fairly easily.

Now, however, it is estimated that there are at least ten million billion billion stars in the known heavens. Counting these would be as impossible as counting all the grains of sand. As a matter of fact, one can show that ten million billion billion is also at least of the order of magnitude of the sand grains of the world (see my commentary, *The Genesis Record*, Baker Book House, 1976, p. 384). This constitutes a remarkable Biblical scientific insight far in advance of its discovery by modern astronomy.

The Bible also says that "one star differeth from another star in glory" (I Corinthians 15:41). To the unaided eye, this statement might also seem questionable. Even with a giant telescope, every individual star appears as a mere point of light in the sky. However, astronomers have found that stars can best be classified by plotting them on a standard graph known as a Hertzsprung-Russell diagram — plotting the star's temperature versus its brightness. When this is done, every star will plot at its own unique point on the diagram — different from all other stars.

Thus each star's "glory" is unique. The Greek world is *doxa*, which specifically means "honor" or "praise." This implies that each star is worthy of its own specific honor and, therefore, must have a specific structure for its own individual divinely ordained function. Since even the nearest star is four light-years distant, it seems hopeless

to think we could ever learn what all these structures and functions might be.

But the Bible clearly teaches that all the stars
of heaven will exist in this same physical universe
forever and ever (see Psalm 148:3-6). In the new
earth, all of the redeemed will have glorified
bodies like that of Christ (see Philippians 3:20,
21). We will no longer be limited by the gravitational and electro-magnetic forces which keep us
earthbound now. We shall have eternity to explore
infinite space. Through the ages to come, we can
learn something of the glory of all the stars.

LIGHT BEFORE THE SUN AND STARS

One of the most common supposed scientific
"errors" in the Genesis account of creation is the
problem of having "light" on Day One (Genesis
1:3-4), whereas the sun and stars were not made
until Day Four (Genesis 1:14-16). The typical
"reconciliation" of this discrepancy is to say that
the cloud cover hiding the sun was removed from
the sky on the fourth day, but this is an arbitrary
and forced interpretation at best.

Evolutionists, for their part, have labored
mightily to contrive a naturalistic explanation of
the development of the sun and stars, but the
best they have come up with so far is the supposed
Primal Big Bang, 18 billion years ago (according to
current speculations), which they think initiated
the subsequent evolution of the universe. Yet, try
as they will to avoid Biblical concepts, they are
compelled to return to them even in formulating
their anti-supernaturalistic models. One of the
world's greatest theoretical physicists, Dr. Victor
F. Weisskopf, recently penned the following

remarkable conclusion to an article entitled "The Origin of the Universe" (*American Scientist*, Vol. 71, 1983, p. 480).

> "Indeed, the Judeo-Christian tradition describes the beginning of the world in a way that is surprisingly similar to the scientific model. Previously it seemed scientifically unsound to have light created before the sun. The present scientific view does indeed assume the early universe to be filled with various kinds of radiation long before the sun was created. 'And God said, Let there be light, and there was light. And God saw the light, that is was good.' "

Now if evolutionary astrophysicists find it necessary to imagine "light" pervading the universe for billions of years before the sun "evolved," those who believe God's Word do not need to equivocate about light being created only three days before the sun! As a matter of fact, God *is* light (I John 1:5), and He didn't have to create it at all. It was the *darkness* that had to be created (Isaiah 45:7).

Of course neither the big bang theory nor any other evolutionary concept of the universe has been proved. Weisskopf admits, "No existing view of the development of the universe is completely satisfactory, and this includes the standard model, . . ." (*Ibid.*, p. 474). All (except direct divine creation in fully developed form, that is) have insuperable difficulties, scientifically as well as Biblically. It is amazing that even when their naturalistic theories impel them in spite of everything back to the Word of God, such scientists still persist in their evolutionary faith.

THE FIZZLING BIG BANG

The generally accepted evolutionary explanation for the origin of the universe has been the so-called "big bang theory," which postulates that a primeval atom exploded about 20 billion years ago and that molecules, stars, galaxies and planets all gradually evolved from the expanding gases of this ancient explosion. Furthermore, the complex molecules that developed from the original exploding particles are said to have slowly evolved into living cells and, finally, into human beings!

This "miracle of the big bang," as British astronomer P.C.W. Davies has called it (*Second Look*, September 1979, p. 27), contradicts at least two basic laws of science:

(1) The second law of thermodynamics states that *"disorder"* in a closed system must increase with time; the "big bang" idea, on the other hand, states that the primeval explosion (which was certainly the *ultimate* in disorder!) has somehow increased the *"order"* of the whole universe with time.

(2) The law of conservation of angular momentum states that pure radial motion (in the primeval explosion, all products must move radially outward from its center) cannot give rise to orbital motion; yet planets, stars and galaxies somehow all managed to start to rotate in vast orbits around different centers throughout the universe.

In spite of these fundamental contradictions, this theory has been accepted by most astronomers and cosmogonists, primarily on the basis of the supposed universal background radiation. This cosmic microwave low-temperature radiation was supposed to be uniform in all directions and thus to represent the remnants of the Big Bang.

Despite its wide acceptance as the standard evolutionary cosmogony, however, some of the best astronomers have remained unconvinced. Hannes Alfven, for example, after a devastating critique of the standard interpretation of this radiation, concluded: "The claim that this radiation lends strong support to hot big bang cosmologies is without foundation" (*Nature*, April 21, 1977, p. 698).

More recently, evidence has been accumulating that the background radiation is not "homogeneous and isotropic," as required by the "big bang theory," but varies in all directions! A recent article concludes: "A quadrupole anisotropy (difference in four directions at right angles to each other) has to belong to the substance of the radiation of the universe itself" (*Science News*, Vol. 119, May 1981, p. 254). This means that this supposedly "uniform" radiation is actually *non-uniform* in all directions, and this is not possible in the big-bang theory.

Thus the "big bang theory" should soon be joining the late-lamented "steady state theory" on the scrap heap of discarded theories of the evolution of the universe.

EVOLUTION FROM NOTHING

Evolutionists have frequently criticized creationism as unscientific because of its basic commitment to the doctrine of creation *ex nihilo* — that is, "creation out of nothing." The idea that God simply called the universe into existence by His own power, without using any pre-existing materials, is rejected out of hand by evolutionists, since this would involve supernatural action, which is unscientific by definiton (that is, by *their* definition).

Yet now we hear many evolutionary astrophysicists maintaining that the universe *"evolved"* itself out of nothing! Creationists at least assume an adequate Cause to produce the universe — that is, an infinite, omnipotent, omniscient transcendent self-existing personal Creator God. For those who believe in God, creation *ex nihilo* is plausible and reasonable. But even if people refuse to acknowledge a real Creator, they should realize that a universe evolving out of nothing would contradict the law of cause-and-effect, the principle of conservation of mass/energy, the law of increasing entropy, and the very nature of reason itself. How can they say such things?

Yet, listen, for example, to Edward P. Tryon, Professor of Physics at the City University of New York, one of the first to propound this idea:

> "In 1973, I proposed that our Universe had been created spontaneously from nothing (*ex nihilo*), as a result of established principles of physics. This proposal variously struck people as preposterous, enchanting, or both" (*New Scientist,* Vol. 101, March 8, 1984, p. 14).

Naturally it would! But a decade later it has become semi-official "scientific" doctrine, and cosmogonists are taking it quite seriously.

For many years, the accepted evolutionary cosmogony has been the so-called big-bang theory. However, there have always been many difficulties with this concept, one of which is to explain how the primeval explosion could be the cause of the complexity and organization of the vast cosmos, and another of which is to explain how a uniform explosion could generate such a non-uniform universe. Creationists have been stressing these problems for years, but now evolutionists themselves are beginning to recognize them.

> "There is no mechanism known as yet that would allow the Universe to begin in an arbitrary state and then evolve to its present highly-ordered state" (Don H. Page, "Inflation Does Not Explain Time Asymmetry," *Nature*, Vol. 304, July 7, 1983, p. 40).

> "The cosmological question arises from cosmologists' habit of assuming that the universe is homogeneous. Homogeneity is known to be violated on the small scale by such things as galaxies and ordinary clusters, but cosmologists held out for a large-scale over-all homogeneity. Now if a supercluster can extend halfway around the sky, there doesn't seem too much room left to look for homogeneity" (D.E. Thomsen, "Hyper-superduper Galaxy Cluster," *Science News*, Vol. 122, December 18/25, 1982, p. 391).

There are many other difficulties with the big bang model, but evolutionary theorists have had nothing better to offer, especially since the abandonment of the rival steady-state theory several years ago.

Sir Fred Hoyle, outstanding astronomer and cosmologist, who finally gave up the steady-state theory which he had originated and long pro-moted, has also shown that the big bang theory should be abandoned, for still other reasons.

> "As a result of all this, the main efforts of investigators have been in papering over holes in the big bang theory, to build up an idea that has become ever more complex and cumbersome . . . I have little hesitation in saying that a sickly pall now hangs over the big bang theory. When a pattern of facts become set against a theory, experience shows that the theory rarely recovers" (The Big Bang under Attack," *Science Digest*, Vol. 92, May 1984, p. 84).

THE INFLATIONARY UNIVERSE

But now, in a new attempt to overcome some of the difficulties of the big bang theory, an amazing new concept has been promoted, a concept known as the "inflationary universe," associated especially with the name of Alan Guth. This is strictly a mathematical construct, impossible even to visualize, let alone test, but its advocates claim that it can resolve the problems posed by the initial stages of the big bang. Its essentials are outlined in the following remarkable scenario:

> "Our present understanding now leads us to the belief that sometime around 10^{-35} second the rate of expansion underwent a dramatic, albeit temporary, increase, to which we apply the term *inflation*. The physical processes that took place during the unification of the strong force with the others caused the universe to expand from a size much smaller than a single proton to

something approximately the size of a grapefruit in about 10^{-35} second" (James Trefil, "The Accidental Universe," *Science Digest,* Vol. 92, June 1984, p. 54).

Now 10^{-35} second is one hundred millionth of a billionth of a billionth of a billionth of a second, whatever that can possibly mean. These inflationary cosmogonists are telling us that, at the beginning, the entire universe (of space, time and matter) was concentrated as an infinitesimal particle, about the size of an electron, with all force systems (gravity, electro-magnetic, nuclear and weak forces) unified as a single type of force. This "universe" somehow went through an inconceivably rapid inflationary stage, reaching grapefruit size in 10^{-35} second, by which time the four forces had become separate forces, the heterogeneities had been generated which would eventually become expressed in the heterogeneous nature of the expanded universe, and the universe was ready to enter the "normal" phase of its big bang. Thus as Tryon says, "In this scenario, the 'hot big bang' was preceded by a 'cold big whoosh' " (E.P. Tryon, *op cit,* p. 16).

To comprehend the arguments behind this inflationary model of the early cosmos, one would require a background in advanced mathematical physics, and not even those who have such a background all accept the model. As the very title of Page's previously cited article states, inflation does not explain time asymmetry. That is, it still contradicts the principle of increasing entropy, or disorder.

"The time asymmetry of the universe is expressed by the second law of thermodynamics, that entropy increases with time as order is transformed into disorder. The mystery is not that an ordered state should become disordered but that the early universe was in a highly ordered state" (D.N. Page, *op cit*, p. 39).

Many, of course, have speculated that the universe as a whole has been eternally oscillating back and forth, so that the inferred point-sized beginning of the expanding universe was merely the hypothetical end result of a previously contracting universe. But this strange notion is clearly not a solution to the entropy problem.

> "We now appreciate that, because of the huge entropy generated in our Universe, far from oscillating, a closed universe can only go through one cycle of expansion and contraction. Whether closed or open, reversing or monotonically expanding, the severely irreversible phase transitions transpiring give the universe a definite beginning, middle and end" (S.A. Bludman, "Thermodynamics and the End of a Closed Universe," *Nature*, Vol. 308, March 22, 1984, p. 322).

In fact, Bludman, who is in the Department of Physics at the University of Pennsylvania, also makes the following fascinating comment:

> "Finally, we show that if space is closed and the Universe began with low entropy, then it had to begin, not with a hot big bang, but with a non-singular tepid little bang" (*Ibid.*, p. 319).

If the universe is "open," then its inferred expansion should go on forever, but if it is closed, and eventually begins to fold back in on itself, then it could never bounce back again. It would end in a "final crunch," says Bludman.

Which brings our discussion back again to the remarkable beginning assumed by the inflationary model. Where did the initial "point-universe" come from? This amazing point-sized particle which somehow contained the entire universe and, in principle, all its future galaxies, planets and people — how do we account for *it*? Now, if one thinks that the scenario up to this point has been enchantingly preposterous, he will surely think the rest of it is simply a creationist plot to make evolutionists look ridiculous! Readers should certainly check this out for themselves.

How did it all come to pass? Edward Tryon, who started many of these metaphysical exercises back in 1973, says: "So I conjectured that our Universe had its physical origin as a quantum fluctuation of some pre-existing true vacuum, or state of nothingness" (Tryon, *op cit.* p. 15). So our vast, complex cosmos began as a point of something or other which evolved as a fluctuation from a state of nothingness!

> "In this picture, the universe came into existence as a fluctuation in the quantum-mechanical vacuum. Such a hypothesis leads to a view of creation in which the entire universe is an accident. In Tryon's words, 'Our universe is simply one of those things which happen from time to time' " (J. Trefil, *op cit*, p. 101).

Lest any readers begin to wonder, this discussion

is not intended as a satire. It is a straightforward recital of what modern astrophysical cosmogonists are proposing as the beginning of our universe. Guth and Steinhardt, two of the most active and ingenious workers in this field, say:

> "From a historical point of view probably the most revolutionary aspect of the inflationary model is the notion that all the matter and energy in the observable universe may have emerged from almost nothing. . . . The inflationary model of the universe provides a possible mechanism by which the observed universe could have evolved from an infinitesimal region. It is then tempting to go one step further and speculate that the entire universe evolved from literally nothing" (Alan H. Guth and Paul J. Steinhardt, "The Inflationary Universe," *Scientific American,* Vol. 250, May 1984, p. 128).

Regardless of the sophisticated mathematical calculations leading the inflationary-universe astronomers to their remarkable statement of faith in the omnipotence of nothingness, there will continue to be a few realists who prefer the creationist alternative: "In the beginning God created the heaven and the earth."

THE REAL WITNESS OF GEOLOGY

The study of the "history" of the earth ("historical" geology) is crucial in correlating science with the Bible. Since evolutionists have no legitimate scientific evidence for evolution as such, they have lately been concentrating their arguments against creation primarily around the Biblical doctrine of *recent* creation, alleging that the earth is billions of years old rather than the few thousand years recorded in Scripture.

IMPORTANCE FOR AN EFFECTIVE CHRISTIAN TESTIMONY

We have already stressed the vital importance of the recent creation doctrine (see Chapter I, pp. 39-46). The evidence shows there is no legitimate way by which the Bible record can be harmonized with the evolutionary ages of the so-called historical geologists. One of these systems must be wrong, and the Christian ought to be willing to stand on the Lord's side in this definitive battle, regardless of the weight of scholarly opinion on the other side.

This question of the nature and duration of earth "history" is actually a touchstone, the issue that really determines a Christian's attitude toward Biblical authority. Compromise on the first chapter of the Bible will inevitably lead to compromise on later chapters, since everything later builds on the Genesis foundation. In fact, reluctance to face this issue is almost certainly the underlying, perhaps subconscious, reason why so many Christians still seem indifferent to the entire creation/evolution conflict.

It is urgent, therefore, to get Christian people to see that the actual facts of geology and other historical sciences will fit perfectly in the literal Biblical framework for earth history, so there is really no excuse for these dangerous compromises to continue. It is probably realistic to say that, if just the Bible-believing Christian community would accept and actively promote the many strong evidences (both Biblical and scientific) for recent creation and flood geology, the entire facade of "scientific" evolution would soon collapse.

This does not mean that evolutionary humanism would vanish as a philosophy, of course, since it has been the essence of all pantheistic and polytheistic religions and philosophical systems throughout history and will continue to be so until Christ returns. But it would mean that its pseudo-scientific veneer would be gone, and evolution would have to stand strictly on its own merits as a religion.

The question that needs to be addressed by the Christian community is simply whether the Bible or evolutionary scientism is to govern our Christ-centered understanding of earth history. The Bible clearly teaches that all things were created and made by the Lord Jesus Christ in six real days several thousand years ago, followed 1656 years later by a world-destroying catclysmic deluge accompanied by extensive volcanic eruptions, earth movements and other geophysical upheavals. Evolutionary geologists for almost 200 years have denied these Biblical doctrines, maintaining that the earth is very old (current estimate is 4.6 billion years), and that its "history" has been dominated by natural uniform processes, with no such event as a global cataclysm to disturb its long slow, evolutionary changes.

If the Bible is really the Word of God, then its record is true and clear. That can only mean that, if all geological data are accurate and correctly understood, they must correlate with the Biblical framework better than with evolutionary long-ages geology. That this is actually the case is the contention of modern Christian creationist scientists.

THE DECLINE AND FALL OF UNIFORMITARIANISM

As a matter of fact, this famous geological principle of uniformitarianism, accepted as dogma by practically all geologists for 150 years, has lately fallen on hard times, along with gradualism in evolutionary biology.

The September 1982, issue of *Geology* contained an important article by James H. Shea, "Twelve Fallacies of Uniformitarianism." Such an article would never have been accepted for publication until very recently. The great Yale geologist, Carl Dunbar, once said, as quoted in *Historical Geology:*

> "This philosophy, which came to be konwn as the doctrine of *unifor-mitarianism,* demands an immensity of time; it has now gained universal acceptance among intelligent and informed people" (Wiley, 1960, p. 18).

The uniformitarian principle has held that "the present is the key to the past" and that, therefore, the various geological records of earth history must be explained entirely by geological processes operating in the past just as they do today. Catastrophes and cataclysms were not supposed to leave any geological records, since they would not have occupied enough time to satisfy the needs of gradual evolution.

However, geologists are now acknowledging that uniformitarianism does not work any better in evolutionary geology than gradualism does in evolutionary biology. Shea says, "The idea that the rates or intensities of geologic processes have

been constant is so obviously contrary to the
evidence that one can only wonder at its per-
sistence." As far as the presumed "immensity of
time" is concerned, Shea says, "Modern uniformitarianism . . . asserts nothing about the age of
Earth or about anything else."

This does not mean, of course, that modern
geologists are becoming creationists, any more
than the new ideas of "punctuated equilibrium"
are making creationists out of modern biologists.
As a matter of fact, the two groups have been
joining forces in the new emphasis on
"revolutionary evolutionism." They are now
crediting great catastrophic geologic upheavals
which may occur from time to time with
stimulating the punctuational advances in
evolution which the new biologists have
proposed.

Just *how* the one generates the other, of
course, remains to be discovered. All *known*
catastrophes produce disorder in previously
ordered systems — not order in previously
disordered systems. But maybe catastrophes
operated under different rules in the past, or so
they seem to hope.

Now Shea was not, by any means, the first
modern evolutionary geologist to question the
traditional geological dogma of uniformitarianism. Paul Krynine, of Penn State, had
long ago called it a "dangerous doctrine" which
was "verily contradicted by all post-Cambrian
sedimentary data" (*Paleontology*, Vol. 30, 1956,
p. 1004). J.W. Valentine, of the University of
California at Davis, had said that its watchword
("the present is the key to the past") was "a
maxim without much credit" (*Journal of
Geological Education*, Vol. XIV, April 1966, p. 60).

Beginning in 1965, Stephen Jay Gould published a whole series of papers, in various journals, attacking uniformitarianism. Derek Ager, Head of Geology, University College of Swansea, and president of the British Geological Association, published an important book in 1973, *The Nature of the Stratigraphical Record* (Wiley, 114 pp.) and then an expanded edition in 1981. The entire book was an indictment of uniformitarianism, insisting that only catastrophism could account for the structures and systems of the geological record. And there were many others.

Nevertheless, uniformitarianism continued to dominate standard geological thought and teaching until very recently, and the Shea article (Shea is editor of the *Journal of Geological Education*) seems perhaps to have been a catalyst. In any case, suddenly the entire geological community seems to have swung over to what might be called neo-catastrophism. Still unwilling to accept again the catastrophism of the Bible and of the founding fathers of geology, centered in the Noahic deluge, the emphasis currently is on the necessity of postulating all sorts of other catastrophes (asteroids, meteorites, comets, volcanoes, regional floods, slipping crusts, splitting continents, sudden pole reversals, and other such phenomena) to explain practically all geological data. Two recent summaries may be taken as typical. Reviewing a recent meeting, Dr. Roger Lewin says:

> " 'It is a great philosophical breakthrough for geologists to accept catastrophism as a normal part of earth history.' This comment, made by Erle

Kauffman at a meeting on the dynamics
of extinction held recently at Northern
Arizona University, Flagstaff, identifies a
currently important, perhaps revolutionary, shift in collective professional
perspectives among paleontologists as
well as geologists. . . . The new
catastrophism, if such an emotive
phrase can be permitted, for many would
disavow the designation, merely allows
for asteroid impact as one of many
agents that from time to time profoundly
perturb global conditions important to
life, including atmospheric and oceanic
circulation, temperature gradient, and
sea level" (*Science*, Vol. 221, September
2, 1983, p. 935).

One of the men largely responsible for this
remarkable new science of the "dynamics of
extinction" is Dr. David Raup, Head of Geology of
the University of Chicago and Curator of geology
at the Field Museum. He says:

"A great deal has changed, however, and
contemporary geologists and paleontologists now generally accept
catastrophism as a 'way of life,' although
they may avoid the word catastrophe. In
fact, many geologists now see rare,
short-lived events as being the principal
contributors to geologic sequences. . . .
The periods of relative quiet contribute
only a small part of the record" (*Field
Museum of Natural History Bulletin*, Vol.
54, March 1983, p. 21).

Geological uniformitarianism, which creationists have been vigorously opposing for over
50 years, has thus suddenly been all but abandoned by the geologists themselves, so there is
hardly any point anymore in citing the many
weaknesses of the concept or the numerous
evidences of catastrophe in the rock strata. For
those wanting more documentation, the ICR
Technical Monograph, *Catastrophes in Earth
History,* by Dr. Steven Austin (1983, 318 pp.)
contains extensive annotated bioliographies on
this neo-catastrophist movement among evolutionary geologists.

CATASTROPHISM AND EVOLUTION

Perhaps it is because evolutionists have been,
for 150 years, so singularly unsuccessful at
learning the mechanics of evolution, that they
are now turning to the "dynamics of extinction."
In any case, the recent abandonment of
gradualism in biological evolution has coincided
with the recent abandonment of gradualism in
geological evolution. Punctuationism (rapid
evolution in a small population) has come into
vogue in biology, concurrently with neo-
catastrophism in geology, and it is naturally very
tempting to relate — or even to equate — the
two. Many contemporary evolutionists are doing
just that, though with reservations.

For example, T.H. Van Andel commented
several years ago, after first pointing out that the
geological record is essentially one of rare
catastropic events separated by long gaps when
nothing much was happening:

"Among the many ideas fermenting
today in the study of evolution there is

one, frequently heard, that ascribes the
major evolutionary steps to a jump
advance, a concentration of major
change in a very brief interval of time.
There seems to be no good reason why
such pulses of evolutionary change
should coincide with the major rare
events that built the sedimentary
sequence in which the record of evolution is contained. Thus, the new
'catastrophist' view of the sedimentary
record implies that key elements of the
evolutionary record may be forever out
of reach" (*Nature,* Vol. 294, December 3,
1981, p. 398).

This pessimistic view concerning the
impossibility of ever learning how evolution worked
was written before the even more recent
"discovery" by Raup and Sepkowski that massive
extinctions have occurred at what they interpreted to be 26 million-year intervals throughout
geologic history (it has since been shown that the
statistical controls on this study were so weak as
to disqualify its conclusions).

In any case, the fossils do seem to record many
extinctions (e.g., the dinosaurs), so evolutionists
are suddenly hopeful that this may somehow provide the key to the evolution of life. Michael
Benton, in the Zoology Department at Oxford
University, has said:

"There is increasing evidence that major
physical changes have caused more
large-scale evolutionary changes than
has competition. . . . Competition may
increase the probability of extinction of
a particular lineage, but it will rarely be

the sole cause, whereas it could be postulated that a catastrophic change in the physical environment is sufficient on its own" ("Large-Scale Replacements in the History of Life," *Nature,* Vol. 302, March 3, 1983, pp. 16, 17).

Likewise, Roger Lewin, of the American Association for Advancement of Science, comments on the necessity — but the overwhelming difficulty — of trying to relate evolutionary advances to geologic catastrophes:

"Each mass extinction in a sense resets the evolutionary clock and so makes the history of life strikingly spasmodic and governed by a greater element of chance than is palatable in strict uniformitarianism. . . . The notorious paucity of the fossil record combines with a greatly varying sedimentation rate to make time resolution of faunal changes little short of a nightmare" ("Extinctions and the History of Life," *Science,* Vol. 221, September 2, 1983, p. 935).

At the 1983 annual meeting of the Geological Society of America, held in Indianapolis, there seemed to be, especially among the paleontologists, an overwhelming consensus developing that catastrophes and their accompanying mass extinctions somehow hold the key to understanding evolution. Dr. Stephen Gould, describing this development with his enthusiastic endorsement, reported:

"There . . . a group of my colleagues in paleontology began to dismantle an old order of thinking about old objects, and

> to construct a new and striking approach
> to a major feature of life's history on
> earth: mass extinction. . . . mass extinc-
> tions have been more frequent, more
> unusual, more intense (in numbers
> eliminated), and more different (in effect
> versus the patterns of normal times)
> than we had ever suspected" (*Natural
> History*, February 1984, p. 14).

Now, mass extinctions — unusual, intense,
different — correlate nicely with the expected
effects of the Genesis flood, but it is difficult to
see how extinctions can tell us anything about
evolution. The extinction of life would seem to be
the polar opposite of the evolution of life. Even if
we could determine for sure, say, that an asteroid
impact resulted in the extinction of the
dinosaurs, this would tell us nothing whatever
about how they evolved in the first place. Nevertheless, Gould wistfully clings to this hope:

> "Heretofore, we have thrown up our
> hands in frustration at the lack of
> expected pattern in life's history — or we
> have sought to impose a pattern that we
> hope to find on a world that does not
> really display it. . . . If we can develop a
> general theory of mass extinction, we
> may finally understand why life has
> thwarted our expectations — and we
> may even extract an unexpected kind of
> pattern from apparent chaos" (*Ibid.*,
> p. 23).

Well, "hope clings eternal," and to the evolutionists anything is apparently preferable to
believing God's record of earth history. Never-

theless, Gould is here retreating again to his Marxist faith that chaos and destruction in some utterly mystic way somehow generate higher order and a better society. In any case, this absurd current notion of evolution generated suddenly by catastrophism, extinction, chance preservation, and quantum speciation of hopeful monsters speaks more loudly than any creationist critique could do, of the utter hopelessness of the scientific case for evolution.

STOP CONTINENTAL DRIFT

Not because it is particularly germane to the creation/evolution question, or even the age of the earth, but because it has so capitvated the popular imagination, it is worth while to inject here a few words of caution about the current concept of continental drift, with all the accompanying scenario of sea-floor spreading, magnetic reversals, plate tectonics, and other phenomena. This is a very far-reaching model — or even a paradigm — but it is much like evolution. That is, it is so flexible that anything can be made to fit it, and it is therefore non-testable. R.A. Lyttelton, one of the world's outstanding astro/geophysicists, has called attention to this weakness:

> "As for the vast verbal and pictorial literature of plate tectonics, with its large number of purely asseverated assumptions, it may surprise some to learn that it simply fails to qualify as a scientific theory. I am sure Jeffries fully agrees with this. Long ago, the great

> Poincare explained that such descriptive
> accounts are not the role of physical
> theories, which should not introduce as
> many or more arbitrary constants (or
> verbal assumptions) as there are
> phenomena to be accounted for; they
> should establish connections between
> different experimental facts, and above
> all they should enable predictions to be
> made" (*Nature,* Vol. 305, October 20,
> 1983, p. 672).

The continental drift-plate tectonics paradigm
does *not* yield "predictions" that can be tested
experimentally, but only "retrodictions" at best,
which may possibly fit the model, of course, since
it is so completely plastic and allows as many
modifying assumptions as may be needed to
make it fit. Lyttelton gives both in this article and
elsewhere many examples of the weakness of this
concept, especially in explaining past periods of
mountain building. Sir Harold Jeffries, who is also
one of the world's top astro/geophysicists, whom
Lyttelton mentioned, also still rejects the whole
idea, for many good reasons, as do various other
competent geologists and geophysicists.

The nearest thing to an experiemental test of
the idea would be an actual measurement of the
distance between two continents, to see whether
that distance is changing. This has recently
become possible by the development of
astronomical interferometers. So far, the results
have been negative.

> "Interferometry is a technique for
> combining signals received
> simultaneously from a given
> astronomical source at two or more

different telescopes. . . . They have done geodetic and astronometric measurements since 1979 and in that time have noticed no significant changes in the distances between the telescopes. Theories of continental drift and gravity theories in which the earth expands over time would expect change" (*Science News*, Vol. 123, January 8, 1983, p. 20). "Meanwhile, since the continents drift as slowly as one's fingernails grow — from one to ten centimeters per year — even the most precise surveying methods available today have not yet detected drift" (Robert Dietz, "In Defense of Drift," (*The Sciences*, Vol. 23, November/December 1983, p. 26).

This negative result, of course, does not prove the continents have not drifted in the past. Nor, for that matter, would any future positive result prove they *did* drift in the past. Even if they did, it would not prove they did not drift much faster in the past. The problem is that the whole concept is simply too flexible to be testable.

It is, in the meantime, unnecessary for Christians to take any specific position on this subject, since it does not affect the creation/evolution issue or the interpretation of the Biblical record one way or the other. When it is incorporated as an integral part of the long-age evolutionary model, of course, as some have done, then it can and should be rejected.

THE DATING GAME

Mark Twain, with his inimitable cynicism, has interpreted the geologist's (especially the Chris-

tian uniformitarian geologist's) belief that he
could date the various events in the supposedly
pre-human aeons of the earth's history, in the
following picturesque fashion:

> "If the Eiffel Tower were now represent-
> ing the world's age, the skin of the paint
> of the pinnacle knob at its summit would
> represent man's share of that age, and
> anybody would perceive that that skin
> was what the tower was built for. I
> reckon they would. I dunno" (*The Damned
> Human Race*, quoted by Robert L. Bates,
> *Geotimes*, Vol. 29, June 1984, p. 54).

That is, if God really took billions of years to
create human beings, and if His purpose really
had been to create people in His own image, and
then to redeem them from sin for fellowship with
Himself (and this is what Christian evolutionists
and progressive creationists must believe), then
what took Him so long, and what was the point?
What an indictment against God's wisdom and
power and love! And what a testimony to human
arrogance — that latter-day evolutionists could
really presume to give the lie to God and try to
date events that they prefer to think took place
billions of years before the beginning of recorded
history and billions of years before God, by divine
revelation, said He created the universe (Exodus
20:8-11; Mark 10:16; etc.).

In this section, therefore, we need to discuss
briefly the invalid assumptions on which the
evolutionists base their estimates for the age of
the earth and the various evolutionary
geological ages.

HOW TO "DATE" A ROCK

The oldest dates in recorded history (that is, as based on written records) are based on the ancient chronologies preserved by the Egyptians, Sumerians and other ancient peoples, including the Biblical chronology itself. At the very most, these only go back several thousand years, perhaps ten thousand at the most, with the more conservative interpretations of these data yielding less than six thousand years.

Where, then, do geologists obtain "dates" in the millions and billions of years? How is a particular rock or fossilized bone dated and placed in proper evolutionary sequence? The average layman tends to think rocks are dated by radiocarbon or some other radioactive mineral, and then the fossils are assigned a date corresponding to the age of the rocks where they are found, which then permits them to be placed in their proper evolutionary sequences.

But it is not like that at all. Derek Ager, past president of the British Geological Association, tells it like it is:

> "No paleontologist worthy of the name would ever date his fossils by the strata in which they are found. It is almost the first thing I teach my first-year students. Ever since William Smith at the beginning of the 19th century, fossils have been and still are the best and most accurate method of dating and correlating the rocks in which they occur. . . . Apart from very 'modern' examples, which are really archaeology, I can think of no cases of radioactive decay being used to date fossils" ("Fossil Frustrations," *New*

Scientist, Vol. 100, November 10, 1983, p. 425).

Thus, fossils are *not* dated by the rocks in which they are found; rather, the rocks are "dated" and correlated by the fossils found in them.

But what is there about the fossils that enables stratigraphers to date rocks with them? Although many people find this hard to believe (or to admit), rocks are "dated" on the basis of the stage of evolution of their fossils — especially their assemblage of "index fossils." For any who question this fact, the following authoritative statements are listed, all from leading geologists:

> "Historic geology relies chiefly on paleontology, the study of fossil organisms. . . . The geologist utilizes knowledge of organic evolution, as preserved in the fossil record, to identify and correlate the lithic records of ancient time." (O.D. von Engeln and K.E. Caster, *Geology,* McGraw-Hill, 1952, p. 423).

> "The only chromometric scale applicable in geologic history for the stratigraphic classification of rocks and for dating geologic events exactly is furnished by the fossils. Owing to the irreversibility of evolution, they offer an unambiguous time-scale for relative age determinations and for world-wide correlations of rocks" (O.H. Schindewolf, *American Journal of Science,* Vol. 255, June 1957, p. 394).

> "Merely in their role as distinctive rock

constituents, fossils have furnished,
through their record of the evolution of
life on this planet, an amazingly effective
key to the relative positioning of strata
in widely separated regions and from
continent to continent" (H.D. Hedberg,
*Bulletin of the Geological Society of
America,* Vol. 72, April 1961, p. 499).

Although the above references are old, they are
not outdated, for this method of geological
"dating" has been in use for 100 years and is still
standard. Rocks are assigned a geologic age
based essentially on the stage-of-evolution of
their fossils. Such a method, of course, has to
assume that evolution is a known fact and its
various stages, with their respective forms of life,
already settled.

But how could all this be known, if it all took
place millions of years ago? As we have seen,
there is no evidence of any vertical evolution
occurring today, nor are there any evolutionary
intermediates in the billions of known fossils
from the past.

As hard as it may be to believe at this late date,
the fact is that most of these imaginary evolutionary stages were originally developed deduc-
tively in the nineteenth century by studies of
comparative morphology and physiology of
existing animals, especially utilizing inferences
drawn from Ernst Haeckel's infamous "recapitulation theory." Stephen Jay Gould referred to this
fact in his study of the racist implications of this
theory, as discussed earlier.

"In Down's day, the theory of recapitulation embodied a biologist's best guide
for the organization of life into

> sequences of higher and lower forms"
> (*Natural History,* April 1980, p. 144).

But the recapitulation theory has long since been proved false, so how could it have been a reliable guide for determining evolutionary sequences? Many people, of course, have maintained that the fossil record gives an actual documented history of evolution, but we have just seen that the so-called fossil record is based on the assumption of evolution and is then used to date the rocks to provide the framework of "history" in which to interpret and correlate them as an evolutionary series.

Naturally, creationists have long insisted that this entire system is a classic case of circular reasoning, and evolutionists are finally admitting it. Raup says, for example:

> "The charge that the construction of the geologic scale involves circularity has a certain amount of validity. . . . Thus, the procedure is far from ideal and the geologic ranges of fossils are constantly being revised (usually extended) as new occurrences are found" (David M. Raup, "Geology and Creation," *Field Museum of Natural History Bulletin,* Vol. 54, March 1983, p. 21).

One portion of the geological time scale was, indeed developed by a sort of inductive process, from actual fossil deposits in the rocks. The most recent of the geologic eras, the Cenozoic (involving the Tertiary and Quaternary Periods) was subdivided by Sir Charles Lyell in the early part of the nineteenth century, by a method that was supposed to be quantitative. A leading modern paleontologist and his colleagues have described this process as follows:

> "In about 1830, Charles Lyell . . . developed a biostratigraphic technique for dating Cenozoic deposits based on relative proportions of living and extinct species of fossil mollusks. . . . Strangely, little effort has been made to test this assumption. This failure leaves the method vulnerable to circularity. When Lyellian percentages alone are used for dating, it remains possible that enormous errors will result from spatial variation in the temporal pattern of extinction" (Steven M. Stanley, Warren O. Addicott and Kujotaka Chinzei, "Lyellian Curves in Paleontology: Possibilities and Limitations," *Geology*, Vol. 8, September 1980, p. 422).

Lyell made his original studies almost exclusively on the rocks of the Paris Basin in France, so it was presumptuous to apply this all over the world. As Stanley and his associates point out.

> "One source of error for Lyellian data that may, in general, bias estimates of extinction rates is a failure to recognize living representatives of some fossil species" (*Ibid.,* p. 424).

These and other problems were real fallacies. The authors conclude:

> "Thus our analysis casts doubt on the universal utility of the Lyellian dating method, even for faunas at a single province" (*Ibid.* p. 425).

These Tertiary and Quaternary subdivisions actually represent the most systematic attempt to develop a truly "inductive" (that is, "erect step-by-step from actual data in the field") technique for organizing a portion of the geological age system. This is the most "recent" part of the time scale and thus, presumably, the clearest and best preserved. Yet it did not work even here. The larger divisions, based on the recapitulation theory and other subjective criteria, are thus even less reliable.

Yet geologists still use it. Raup explains:

> "In spite of this problem, the system does work! The best evidence for this is that the mineral and petroleum industries around the world depend upon the use of fossils in dating. . . . I think it quite unlikely that the major mineral and petroleum companies of the world could be fooled" (David M. Raup, *op cit*, p. 21).

Evidently even such a careful and competent geologist as Dr. Raup can apparently be fooled, however. Oil companies only use fossils in dating (actually microfossils) to trace out a given formation in a given region. They could hardly be used to locate oil-bearing rocks associated with a particular geological age, since oil is found in rocks of *all* ages! Actually, oil geologists and other economic geologists do their prospecting for new deposits on the basis of geophysical criteria, not paleontological.

And whatever they use, it is surely wishful thinking to boast that "the system does work," when only about one out of ten (very costly) wildcat oil wells discovers a new pool!

The bottom line is that the geological ages of rocks depend on the assumption of evolution, and that assumption is wrong. That being the case, there is no objective way to determine the geological age of a rock or fossil deposit. Thus, for all that can be proved to the contrary, they could all well be of essentially the *same* age! And that, of course, is exactly what the Bible teaches.

AGE OF
THE SOLAR SYSTEM

As far as the age of the earth itself is concerned, geologists have to use some other method — one which they hope will yield "absolute time," instead of the "relative times" associated with the fossils and the so-called geologic time scale. Astronomers and "planetary scientists" also become involved here, since it is generally assumed that the entire solar system evolved together, perhaps out of an earlier galactic swirling dust cloud, or something of the sort.

The main reason offered for the multi-billion dollar NASA space program was the hope of learning exactly how and when the solar system did "evolve," since our nation's scientific and political establishments were unwilling to believe it happened in the way God said it happened, by special creation of the sun, moon and stars (including planets) on the fourth literal day of creation week (Genesis 1:14-19; Psalm 33:6-9).

Now, with all our space probes, lunar landings, satellites, and other space paraphernalia, we are still no closer to understanding the evolutionary origin of the solar system than we were 20 years ago. Scientists still don't even understand the moon's origin, although it has been the object of more study than any other object in the solar system, except the earth itself. Dr. Michael Drake reports:

> "Although it has been fourteen years since the first lunar samples were returned to Earth by the Apollo mission, the origin of the moon remains unresolved" (Geochemical Constraints on the Origin of the Moon," *Geochimica et Cosmochima Acta*, Vol. 47, 1983, p. 1759).

We know even less about Mars and Venus or the mysterious moons of Jupiter and rings of Saturn, for what *has* been learned in the space program has made their origin and evolution more enigmatic than ever, and the same is true of the asteroids, comets and meteorites. As far as the sun itself is concerned, one very important (but controversial) discovery has some very significant implications.

> "Astronomers were startled and laymen amazed, when in 1979 Jack Eddy, of the High Altitude Observatory in Boulder, Colorado, claimed that the sun was shrinking, at such rate that, if the decline did not reverse, our local star would disappear within a hundred thousand years" (John Gribbin, "The Curious Case of the Shrinking Sun," *New Scientist*, March 3, 1983, p. 592).

This discovery indeed caused shock waves in the scientific community. Its implications were supported by the well-known rarity of solar neutrinos, (high-energy sub-atomic particles supposedly being produced in the sun) whose absence seems to mean that the sun's burning is not being fueled by thermonuclear fusion processes in its interior, as long believed, but by energy derived from its own gravitational collapse as it shrinks.

Since the shrinking rate reported by Eddy meant that the solar system could not possibly be very old — a few hundred thousand years at the most — the idea has been strongly resisted. Subsequent investigations obtained smaller figures for the rate of shrinkage, but did confirm the *fact* of shrinkage. An "over-all decline in solar diameter of about 0.1 seconds of arc per century since the early 1700s is real," based on "a battery of statistical tests," according to astrophysicist Ronald Gilliland (*Ibid.*, p. 594).

This figure was only about 5% of the shrinkage rate obtained by Eddy, and undoubtedly has been made as small as the data would possibly allow, but even this shrinkage rate would mean that the sun would have been about twice its size a million years ago (the time of the supposed Ice Age!).

Such a thing cannot have been, if the standard geological time scale is correct. Nevertheless, that is what the data seem to show.

> "As for the longer-term decline in solar diameter, the discovery that started the whole ball rolling, Gilliland was cautious in his claims. 'Given the many problems with the data sets,' he said, 'one is not inexorably led to the conclusion that a negative secular solar radius trend has existed since A.D. 1700, but the preponderance of current evidence

> indicates that such is likely to be the
> case' " (Ibid., p. 594).

One indeed needs to be cautious when publishing
data that indicate the solar system is young, as
this can be a quick path to academic exile. Dr.
Eddy had already created quite a furor when he
participated in a symposium at Louisiana State
University where several speakers had suggested
that there was at least a possibility that the earth
was still young and very active geophysically. The
purpose of the symposium, organized by Dr.
Raphael G. Kazmann of the engineering faculty,
was to alert scientists to the possibility that
certain proposals for storing radioactive waste
materials in what geologists claimed were very
ancient stable formations might be very
dangerous if the earth actually were still young.
At this symposium, Eddy had said:

> "I suspect that the sun is 4.5 billion
> years old. However, . . . I suspect that we
> could live with Bishop Ussher's value for
> the age of the earth and sun. I don't
> think we have much in the way of obser-
> vational evidence in astronomy to con-
> flict with that" (John A. Eddy, "Time,
> Trees and Solar Change," as reported in
> Geotimes, Vol. 23, September 1978,
> p. 18).

Now, Dr. Eddy is an extremely competent scientist, certainly familiar with all the "observational
evidence in astronomy" that would bear on such
matters. When he and his colleagues at the High
Altitude Observatory conclude that the sun is
shrinking and that there is no good evidence that
it is older than Bishop Ussher's 6000-year figure,
other scientists would do well to listen.

Instead, they write it off as an "oscillation," assuming that the sun alternately shrinks and expands, although they have no idea what could make it do this. This "pulsation" notion is obviously an *ad hoc* hypothesis to save the great age of the earth. Although there are, of course, certain periodic changes in the sun (e.g., sunspots), the sun has been shrinking steadily for the almost 300 years for which measurements are available. *That* is what is known'; the oscillation idea is wishful thinking.

This strong evidence of a young earth and solar system is supported by a great abundance of other evidences which will not be discussed here. My book *The Biblical Basis for Modern Science* (Baker Book House, 1984), has a tabulation of 68 worldwide processes which yield ages far too small to support the standard geological time table or the supposed evolution of life on earth (pp. 477-480). Also see other books listed in the bibliography in Appendix A.

These references may also be consulted for a critique of the standard radiometric dating techniques used in arriving at so-called "absolute time" figures for various igneous rock formations in the geologic column. All of these techniques are based on assumptions which are unprovable, untestable, unreasonable and impossible! They yield a wide scattering of results, with only those retained which conform to what the dates "should" be (circular reasoning again).

Once again there is no reason whatever for Christians to be intimidated by this dating game. The Biblical record of a young earth and worldwide flood fits all the real facts of science. The flood will be further discussed in the next chapter.

Chapter VI

Testimony of the Great Flood

THE REAL MEANING OF THE FOSSILS

There is a gigantic graveyard in the world, one which extends all around the surface of the earth and averages a mile or more in depth. This graveyard contains billions upon billions of the dead remains of animals of all kinds, living and extinct, in addition to the tremendous mats of vegetation which have been converted into the great coal beds of the world, plus the tremendous reservoirs of oil and gas which most geologists believe to be largely the converted organic residue of multitudes of marine plants and invertebrate animals.

This is the fossil "record" of the earth's past history, also known as the geologic column. It rests upon the crystalline "basement complex" of the earth's lower crust, which is a mass of igneous and metamorphic rocks containing no fossils and presumably representing the original materials of the primordial earth. Sometimes this basement is right at the surface, sometimes it is covered with 15 miles or more of sedimentary, fossil-bearing rocks and sediments; but the average overburden is about a mile.

What is the meaning of this vast cemetery?

THE GENESIS FLOOD

To the uniformitarian geologist — as well as to the modern neo-catastrophist geologist — this fossil graveyard represents the earth's presumed 4.6 billion-year sequence of geological ages, recording the story not only of Earth's structural changes during that immense period of time, but (more importantly) the evolutionary history of life on Earth, beginning with the simplest organisms forming out of the primeval soup maybe four billion years ago, then continuing through various developmental stages leading finally to human life appearing at the very tag-end of the geological ages a few million years ago.

This evolutionary scenario, developed in the framework of the supposed geologic ages, is almost universally accepted and taught in the schools and colleges of the world today, and has been so taught for over a hundred years. Yet, as we have seen, it is utterly false, and its propagation has wrought untold harm in human life and society. As we have also seen, the geological ages themselves are based on the assumption of evolution, even though the billions of documented fossils have never yet yielded any evolutionary intermediates in the process of evolving. There is no scientific evidence whatever of real "vertical" evolution — either in the world of the present, the world of the past, or the realm of the possible. And if there is no real evidence of evolution, there is no real evidence of the geological ages, for the two concepts are essentially identical.

But the fossils themselves are real. If they do not represent the geological ages, then what *do* they represent? What *is* the meaning of this immense, worldwide, water-laid graveyard of plants and animals and human beings?

The answer clearly has to be the great Flood, the account of which is recorded in detail in Genesis (Chapters 6-9) and is reflected in the ancient traditions of at least 200 nations and tribes in all parts of the world. The Bible, of course, contains a clear witness to the historical reality of this devastating global hydraulic cataclysm, not only in Genesis but all through Scripture. There are several allusions to it in the ancient book of Job, the psalmists refer to it (especially Psalms 29 and 104), the prophets write of it and of Noah (particularly Isaiah and Ezekiel), and so does the writer of Chronicles. In the new Testament, it is mentioned at least in Matthew, Mark, Hebrews, I Peter, II Peter, and Jude, with several allusions in Revelation.

The Lord Jesus Christ Himself referred to it (Matthew 24:37-39; Luke 17:26, 27), accepting it not only as a fact of history, worldwide in its extent and effects, but even making it a specific type of His promised second coming, which also would be worldwide in its extent and effects. How can Christian leaders dare to suggest that the flood was "local" and/or "tranquil" in the face of these clear teachings from the Lord they profess to serve?

There is an especially cogent passage in the last chapter written by the Apostle Peter just before his execution as a Christian martyr, a chapter revealing a remarkable prophetic foreview of the very issues discussed in this book.

> "Knowing this first, that there shall come in the last days scoffers, walking

> after their own lusts, And saying, Where
> is the promise of His coming? for since
> the fathers fell asleep, all things con-
> tinue as they were from the beginning of
> the creation. For this they willingly are
> ignorant of, that by the word of God the
> heavens were of old, and the earth
> standing out of the water and in the
> water: whereby the world that then was,
> being overflowed with water, perished"
> (II Peter 3:3-6).

This passage was written specifically as a warning and exhortation to Christians, not to the
world at large (note verses 1 and 2), especially
preparing them through the Scriptures for *the
last days,* when even many who know about
Christ and His promises will repudiate both Him
and His Word.

And they will do so on the premise that "all
things continue as they were from the beginning
of the creation." This is as clear and succinct a
statement of naturalistic evolutionary uniformitarianism as one could find, indicating that
they think even "creation" is still "continuing" by
means of the same processes that have always
functioned in the past.

God then charges those who promote this doctrine with "wilful ignorance." That is, there is
overwhelming evidence against the doctrine, and
it is easily available to them, but they refuse to
consider it! This is a precise description of the
situation in science and education (and much
religion) today.

The evidence which they choose to ignore falls
into two major categories:

   (1)   Evidence for special creation, not by

means of processes which "continue,"
but processes initiated and consummated in the creation week by "the word
of God."

(2) Evidence for the worldwide Flood, which
comprised a great "discontinuity" (or
"singularity") In the processes of
conservation which God initiated after
the completion of His creation week. The
passage, literally translated, says that
"the cosmos that then was, being
cataclysmically overwhelmed with
water, died."

We have already surveyed and documented
many of the evidences pertaining to Category 1.
They are, indeed, so strong and so varied that
continued belief in evolution is truly wilful
ignorance. In this final chapter we want to look
briefly at the evidences relating to Category 2,
the great Flood.

According to this prophecy, the Flood (literally
"the cataclysm") was primarily hydraulic in
nature and caused the primeval cosmos ("the
heavens which were of old, and the earth") to
"perish." That is, the pre-Flood atmosphere and
geosphere ("heavens and earth") were destroyed
as a "cosmos" (or ordered system), so that "the
heavens and earth which are now" (verse 7) are
drastically different, with their primeval
perfection and order now disfigured and chaotic
in comparison. Furthermore, the "heavens and
earth" which perished include also, by obvious
implication, the inhabitants of the heavens and
earth, or " sky and land." As it says in Genesis
7:21: "And all flesh died that moved upon the
earth, both of fowl, and of cattle, and of beast,

and of every creeping thing that creepeth upon the earth, and every man."

They were all overflowed with water and thereby perished. Since the agent of destruction was the very "water" in which and out of which the earth was standing (that is the water both under and over the firmament, or expanse of atmosphere, as described in Genesis 1:6-8), the inhabitants of the water did not all perish, but only the inhabitants of the atmosphere (birds, insects, bats, extinct flying reptiles) and of the dry land (land mammals, reptiles, perhaps most amphibians, and especially man), except for those preserved in Noah's Ark.

Now, although none of the Biblical passages mention any of these organisms being preserved as fossils (in fact, the Bible does not mention fossils at all), the fact remains that a hydraulic cataclysm of the dimensions and intensity described in the Bible (when all the floodgates of heaven were opened and all the fountains of the great deep violently erupted, all over the world, continuing at maximum intensity for forty days and forty nights) would necessarily erode and transport great volumes of sediment and thereby bury immense numbers of plants and animals in these sediments when they were later deposited as the flood subsided. Barring miraculous intervention (which is neither mentioned nor hinted) the Genesis Flood would have to have been the most effective agency for the formation of fossil-bearing sedimentary rocks that the world has ever experienced.

Therefore, for geologists — especially Christian geologists — to ignore the Flood in their efforts to reconstruct earth "history" from the fossil "record," is indeed wilful ignorance of a high order. And to say that the Genesis Flood was merely a local flood, or else a worldwide tranquil flood, is altogether inexcusable. A local flood could not cover all the world's mountains for five months (Genesis 7:19-8:4), and a worldwide tranquil flood is a contradiction in terms, like a worldwide tranquil explosion! Does the Lord God laugh in derision at people who propose such things? (Psalm 2:4).

UNITY AND CONTINUITY

It is very important to remember that the geologic "ages" are distinguished from each other *only* by "their" fossils. Although there are many, many different types of rocks and minerals and structural features, they are each and all scattered indiscriminately through the various ages. That is, any so-called geologic age can include shales, basalts, limestones and any other petrologic complex; any geologic age may yield quartz, feldspar, iron, or any other mineral or metal; any geologic age may have rocks containing coal or oil or natural gas; and any age may exhibit any type of fold, fault, intrusion or other structural features. The rocks all seem to be *one* age as far as their physical and chemical characteristics are concerned.

It is even more important to note that the *only* global unconformity in the geologic column occurs right at the bottom of the column, where it rests on the crystalline basement. What this means is that the sedimentation process which deposited the sediments which eventually became the sedimentary rocks which make up the geologic column was continuous, from bottom to top, without a break.

Now, an "unconformity" is the contact surface

between two rock formations (say, for example, where a shale formation overlies a sandstone formation) when the sediments above and below the surface do not "conform" to each other in terms of the direction of the strata (or "layers" of sediment) which comprise the two formations. Flat-lying strata may overlie a set of planed-off inclined strata, for instance, with the interface surface between the two sets called an unconformity.

The significance of all this is that an unconformity surface represents an erosional surface and, therefore, an unknown lapse of time between the time when the strata of the lower formation stopped being deposited and the strata of the upper formation began to be deposited. An unconformity, in short, represents a time gap in the process of sedimentary deposition when the sediments which would eventually be hardened into sedimentary rocks were first being laid down.

A conformity, on the other hand, is an interface between two formations where the sedimentary strata above and below conform to each other in orientation and angle. The implication in such a case would be that the deposition process was continuous, with the formation above laid down immediately after the one below, with no opportunity for any intervening earth movements or sea-level drop or other physical change to initiate erosion instead of deposition on the surface. There are some conformity surfaces, however, where it is thought a time lapse may have occurred, because of a sudden change in the evolutionary stage of the contained fossils above and below. Such situations are usually called "deceptive conformities" or "paraconformities" but, since their main mark of recognition is the absence of an assumed intervening evolutionary stage, they are questionable, to say the least.

In general, therefore, a conformity surface indicates continuous deposition, while an unconformity indicates a significant gap in time in that part of the geologic column. The missing time may be long or short; there is no way to tell from the unconformity itself.

With this background discussion, it should be easy to see that, if there were such a thing as a worldwide unconformity, say between the Cambrian Period and the Ordovician Period (or any two other geological "ages"), it would be an ideal way of demarking the various geological ages and dating the rocks. As a matter of fact, in the very early days of the development of historical geology, it was actually believed that this was the case.

This idea, however, was abandoned long ago, not only on a worldwide basis, but even on a local basis. Note the following recommendation by two top authorities, written soon after World War II.

> "The employment of unconformities as time-stratigraphic boundaries should be abandoned. Because of the failure of unconformities as time indices, time-stratigraphic boundaries of Paleozoic and later age must be defined by time, — hence by faunas" (H.E. Wheeler and E.M. Beesley, "Critique of the Time-Stratigraphic Concept," *Bulletin of the Geological Society of America*, Vol. 59, 1948, p. 84).

Once again, it is emphasized that rocks are "dated" not by any physical criteria — even such obvious time boundaries as unconformities — but only by fossils, which means evolution.

More important for our immediate discussion, however, is the now-recognized fact that there are no worldwide unconformities (either physical unconformities, or fossil unconformities, for that matter) and therefore no world wide time break in the geologic column.

This means — and this is very important — that *the entire geologic column, all over the world, is a unit, deposited continuously from bottom to top without a time break.* It is a unitary phenomenon, and therefore must have a unitary cause.

The unitary cause can be nothing else than the Genesis Flood, in which, "the world that then was, being overflowed with water, perished." We have already shown that catastrophism is now generally accepted even by most evolutionary geologists. That is, every unit in the geologic column was formed by some kind of "rare event" or "catastrophe" — a local flood, volcanic eruption, landslide, tsunami, or some other violent phenomenon.

Now, if every unit in the geologic column was produced by at least a local catastrophe, and all the units are connected through a continuous deposition process, then the entire series must represent merely different local components of the same worldwide cataclysm. The whole is the sum of its parts.

Even though this chain of reasoning may appear simplistic, it is straightforward and seems compelling, if the assumptions on which it is based are valid. There are really only two assumptions: (1) every formation in the geologic column was formed rapidly, in some kind of catastrophic depositional environment; (2) there is no worldwide unconformity, or time gap in the sedimentary fossil-bearing geologic column.

There are still some die-hard uniformitarians who would question the first assumption but, as documented in the preceding chapter, more and more in the modern school of geologists are saying that everything in the geologic column is a record of catastrophe. Derek Ager, for example has said:

> "To me the whole record is catastrophic, . . . in the sense that only the episodic events — the occasional ones — are preserved for us" (In symposium, *Catastrophes and Earth History*, ed. by W.A. Berggren and J.A. Van Couvering, Princeton University Press, 1984, p. 93).

Ager also has written:

> "The history of any one of the earth, like the life of a soldier, consists of long periods of boredom and short periods of terror" (*The Nature of the Stratigraphic Record*, Wiley, 1981, p. 107).

This last quotation was the last sentence of his book, summarizing its entire message. Ager, of course, does not believe that the "short periods of terror" all represent the Biblical Flood. In fact, he says that the individual catastrophes were "short 'happenings' interrupting long ages of nothing in paticular" (*Ibid.*, p. 99). Similarly, Robert Dott, in his June 1982 presidential address to the Society of Economic Paleontologists and Mineralogists, said:

> ". . . the sedimentary record is largely a record of episodic events. . .episodicity is the rule, not the exception" (*Geotimes*, November 1982, p. 16).

As far as the second assumption is concerned, practically all geologists would agree that there are no worldwide unconformities in the so-called Phanerozoic part of the geologic column, but a few still would say that a global unconformity exists at the base of the Cambrian system, supposedly the oldest of the geological ages with multi-cellular life forms. In the Precambrian (Proterozoic Era) there are great thicknesses of sedimentary rocks but for a long time it was believed there were no fossils in these rocks. Later many reports began to come in of different deposits of protozoan fossils (one-celled organisms) in the Precambrian, but many still believed there was a worldwide unconformity between the Precambrian and Cambrian.

In recent years, however, there have been several sites around the world where an odd assortment of soft-bodied multi-celled animals have been found in Precambrian rocks. These are known as the Ediacaran fauna, named after the Australian site where they were first discovered. A particularly significant site has been found in eastern Siberia. In this region are located what so far are considered.

> ". . . the best sequences of rocks spanning the boundary, about 570 million years old, between the Cambrian and Precambrian geological periods" (Cheryl Simon, "In with the Older," *Science News*, Vol. 123, May 7, 1983, p. 300).

A photograph of the site carries the following caption:

> "These rocks along the Aldan River in Siberia span the boundary with little or

> no disruption, and clearly log the
> evolution of shelled animals and their
> soft-bodied antecedents" (*Ibid.*).

The caption is unrealistic in one respect; there
are no intermediate fossils between the Ediacaran
soft-bodied animals and the shelled animals of
the Cambrian. In fact, Adolph Seilacher of
Germany, supported by Stephen Gould and
others, have shown that the Ediacaran fossils
were so different as to be completely unrelated to
the later animals, dying off without descendants
(Stephen J. Gould, *Natural History*, Vol. 93,
February 1984, p. 15).

But in any case, the so-called unconformity did
not exist, at least at ths site in Siberia. The
sediments of the Precambrian are continuous
with those of the Cambrian, so there is, indeed,
no worldwide time break in the sediments of the
geologic column. Now, again, if there is no
universal time gap in the geologic column, and if
all individual formations represent intense
depositional episodes (many geologists still don't
like the word "catastrophe"), then the entire
column must represent *one continuous intense
depositional episode,* a one-of-a-kind "rare event."
And this fits perfectly with the Biblical record
(and worldwide traditions) of the great Flood.

At the very least, this model ought to be given
serious scientific consideration, as a possible
alternative to the failed model of evolutionary
uniformitarianism. Whether evolutionary
scientists are willing to consider it or not,
however (after all, the Apostle Peter did predict
something about wilful ignorance!), Bible-
believing Christians have no legitimate
alternative, and it is hoped and urged that they

begin to take it seriously.

There is a tremendous, though silent, witness — all over the world, in the rocks of the earth's crust everywhere — to the awful fact of God's judgment on a wicked world. Men have corrupted this record into a counterfeit, purporting to depict evolutionary progress over the ages culminating in humanistic glory, instead of the wrath of God on human rebellion. Both Peter and Jesus said the great hydraulic cataclysm was only a type of the fiery cataclysm yet to come, and men and women would be well advised to be willingly responsive to the Word of God, not willingly ignorant.

PROBLEMS IN THE FLOOD MODEL

There are, of course, a number of significant unresolved difficulties in correlating all the geological data with the Biblical record, and there is room for much further creationist research in this field. Nevertheless, these problems are minor compared to those of the evolutionists, and we can at least discern plausible ways in which these problems might be answered even now.

THE SUPPOSED ORDER OF THE FOSSILS

One of the most persuasive arguments of the evolutionists is based on the supposed order of the fossils in the geologic column. At the bottom are the one-celled animals, then the strange soft-bodied Ediacaran assemblage, referred to on pp. 242-243, then the many marine invertebrates of the Cambrian, above them the fishes, then amphibians, then the reptiles, followed by birds and mammals, and finally man. Supposedly, as one moves upward through the sedimentary rocks of the geologic column, he is also progressing forward through the geological "ages."

In spite of the fact that there are no transitional forms in this geologic record, this order of the fossils seems at least to *look* like evolution. "How come there are only marine invertebrates in the Cambrian rocks," they will argue, "if all the animals were really living in the world simultaneously?" "If all these beds were formed by the Genesis Flood, how did they get separated like this into what looks like an evolutionary series?" Why are so many of the animals that are abundant in ancient "periods" (e.g. dinosaurs, therapsids, trilobites) not found in more "recent" rocks, or even still living?

Well, just how *can* we explain the order of the fossils in terms of the Biblical flood, rather than evolution?

In the first place, by stressing that the so-called order of the fossils is mainly an idealized evolutionary construct which doesn't exist at all in the real world!

The standard geologic "column" can be found only in textbooks, not anywhere in the actual rocks. Nowhere is it found even partially complete at any one locality. The standard column would be at least 100 miles high, whereas the average local column is only one mile high.

As we have seen, originally the geologic age system was not based primarily on actual fossil sequences in the rocks, but on the assumption of evolution, as guided by the recapitulation theory (growth of the fetus in the womb going through the past evolutionary stages of the history of life) and other considerations derived from the comparative morphologies (physical characteristics) of existing animals.

There is thus no real evidence of evolutionary order and progress in the rocks. Stephen Jay Gould himself admits this, perhaps inadvertently:

> "As we survey the history of life since the inception of multicellular complexity in Ediacaran times, one feature stands out as most puzzling — the lack of clear order and progress through time among marine invertebrate faunas. We can tell tales of improvement for some groups, but in honest moments we must admit that the history of complex life is more a story of multifarious variation about a set of basic designs than a saga of accumulating excellence. The eyes of early trilobites, for example, have never been exceeded for complexity or acuity by later arthropods. Why do we fail to find this expected order? . . . I regard the failure to find a clear 'vector of progress' in life's history as the most puzzling fact of the fossil record" (*Natural History*, Vol. 93, February 1984, pp. 22, 23).

Similarly, David Raup has pointed out that:

> "The fossil record of evolution is amenable to a wide variety of models ranging from completely deterministic to completely stochastic" (*American Scientist*, Vol. 166, February 1977, p. 57).

That is, the actual fossil sequences can be interpreted in just about any way one desires, all the way from a uniformly changing series to a complete random scattering of fossils. In the same vein, geologists David Kitts pointed out the following:

> "The fossil record doesn't even provide any evidence in support of Darwinian theory except in the weak sense that the fossil record is compatible with it, just as it is compatible with other evolutionary theories, and revolutionary theories, and special creationist theories and even ahistorical theories" (*Paleobiology*, Vol. 5, Summer 1979, p. 354).

More recently, Dr. Raup has made the following very fascinating observations:

> "In the years after Darwin, his advocates hoped to find predictable progressions. In general, these have not been found — yet the optimism has died hard, and some pure fantasy has crept into textbooks."
>
> "One of the ironies of the evolution-creation debate is that the creationists have accepted the mistaken notion that the fossil record shows a detailed and orderly progression and they have gone to great lengths to accommodate this 'fact' in their Flood geology" ("Evolution and the Fossil Record," *Science*, Vol. 213, July 17, 1981, p. 289).

Thus, according to the testimony of these leading evolutionists, there is really little or no evidence of evolutionary progression through the various systems of the geological column. Therefore, there is no need to try to explain this order in terms of the Flood phenomena, since there is no order to explain anyhow. Yet, as we have seen, the different geological "ages" in the column were actually developed on the assumption of an evolutionary progression in the first place.

All of this seems quite confusing, and the entire subject seems in urgent need of clarification. One reasonable suggestion might be that the evolutionary uniformitarian model has failed. The actual rocks and their fossils fit neither uniformitarianism nor evolutionism, and it is high time for the Biblical Flood model at least to be considered.

Most geologists, of course, are not yet willing to go as far as Raup, Gould and Kitts in denying any signficant evolutionary order in the rocks. They still maintain that the standard geological column is a good representaion of actual sequences, so that each local geological column can be placed satisfactorily in the standard column. These are the geologists, of course, who challenge creationists to try to explain this order in terms of the Flood. So — assuming for the sake of argument that some reasonable facsimile of the standard evolutionary order does exist in the actual rocks — how can we explain the fact that all rocks do not contain fossils of all animals in a heterogeneous jumble? And why do the *local* columns seem usually to fit into the standard column?

DEPOSITION IN A GLOBAL FLOOD

To the extent that there really *is* any order in the geologic deposits of each region, the order is generally what would be expected in a worldwide Flood. It is obviously impossible to deduce exactly what would happen when a global hydraulic cataclysm, accompanied by other intense and violent phenomena of all kinds, would descend upon an earth whose surface was vastly different from that on the present earth. Such a unique event is not repeatable or testable in a laboratory.

Nevertheless, there is no reason at all to think that the result would be a mixed-up jumble of all types of fossils in all parts of the world. Local floods don't work that way, nor do other local physical catastrophes. There would surely have to be a definite relation between the types and locations of the deposited fossil-containing sediments, and the types and original locations of the materials and organisms that were submerged and transported by the floodwaters.

Thus, in general, organisms that lived in a given ecological community would tend to be buried in a corresponding ecological assemblage. One would never expect, for example, fossil fish and fossil horses to be found in the same deposit for the obvious reason that they did not live in the same envirnoment.

Floodwaters generally are not *mixing* agents — they are highly efficient *sorting* agents. Even if a very diverse mixture of objects is attacked and transported by water, the flow will normally tend quickly to segregate them into objects of similar size and shape and then finally to deposit them in a well-sorted series of beds. This phenomenon of hydrodynamic sorting is very real, and can be demonstrated both theoretically and experimentally. An indiscriminate mixture of, say, birds and fish and mammals in a fossil deposit would be a very unusual deposit — an exception, not the rule — in the sediments resulting from a worldwide flood. There are such exceptions, of course, and these merely emphasize that the Flood's activities were very complex, with local, temporary pockets of violent action in a broader context of generally regular and predictable action.

This subject could be discussed at great length and there is, indeed, need and opportunity for much fruitful research by creationist geologists in attempting to reconstruct exactly what may have happened in each region of the world as it was being transformed by the Flood from "the world that then was" to "the world that now is." An extensive discussion is given on this subject in the book "The Genesis Flood, by Dr. John Whitcomb and myself (Presbyterian and Reformed Publ. Co., 1961, 518 pp.). A number of other books listed in Appendix A also deal with it.

As a general rule of thumb, it is obvious that — other things being equal — such a Flood would tend to deposit organisms in ecological burial zones corresponding to the ecological life zones where they were living when caught up by the Flood. Thus, organisms living at the lowest elevations (deep-sea marine invertebrates) would be buried at the lowest elevations, while organisms living at higher elevations (bears, birds, etc.) would tend to be deposited at higher elevations. Another factor necessary to consider is that of mobility. Animals that are capable of running, swimming, climbing or flying can escape burial longer than others. One would, for example, expect to find few fossils of birds or human beings for this reason. Even though finally overtaken and drowned in the rising floodwaters, they would be much less likely to be trapped in the sediments and preserved as fossils than other less mobile animals.

In general, therefore, it is clear that a worldwide flood would tend to produce fossil sequences closely approximating those in the standard geological column. There would be many exceptions, of course, and there *are* many exceptions to the standard order, as already discussed.

It should be noted again in this connection that each local geologic column normally incorporates only a few of the geological "periods." If both marine and terrestrial formations are found in the same column, the marine formations usually (as expected) would be on the bottom, land sediments on top. Only rarely is a formation containing fossils of land animals found interspersed between two marine formations from different periods. The main exception to this rule is in the cyclic deposits (e.g., coal seams) along the interface between the lands and the rising waters, as sediments are brought in and deposited first from one direction and then the other. Normally, all these, however, would be from the same geological "period."

Even assuming that each geological deposit was laid down rapidly, as discussed previously, many have argued that it would take great lengths of time to convert these sediments into the solid rocks of the geological column. The great thickness of non-lithified sediments in off-shore delta deposits or deep-sea sediments are offered as cases in point.

However, the rate of lithification (that is, conversion of loose sediment into stone) depends on many variables, chief of which is the presence or absence of a cementing agent, such as calcite, silica or others. In the context of the Flood, such materials would be abundant everywhere. Also there would, of course, be plenty of water, as well as conditions of changing pressure and temperature, all of which are conducive to rapid lithification under the right conditions. As a very relevant example, one need only think of the conversion of a "sediment" of sand, gravel and water (plus cement!) into solid rock (concrete) in a matter of a few hours. This kind of phenomenon would have been common during and after the Flood.

ANOMALIES IN THE GEOLOGIC COLUMN

Another evidence that the standard column is purely an arbitrary construct based on evolution is the fact that exceptions to the standard order are so frequent. Practically every local column has examples of "missing ages" in the sequences, many of which are "paraconformities," (see p. 238) with the missing ages evident only because of the missing fossils. Even more significant are the many examples of "reversed ages," and "old" formations resting conformably on "young" formations.

The most basic rule of stratigraphy (the study of the sequences of "strata," or layers, in the rocks) is that sedimentary rock formations on the bottom are older than those on the top. Sedimentary rocks are formed by the erosion, transportation, and deposition of sediments, and nothing could be more obvious than the fact that deposits on top were laid down after the sediments below them. However, this common-sense rule often seems not to work.

> "In many places, the oceanic sediments of which mountains are composed are inverted, with the older sediments lying on top of the younger" (*Science News*, V. 98. October 17, 1970, p. 316).

If this is the case, then how did those in authority ever decide that the bottom rocks were younger. The answer is that, as already discussed, they are dated by the fossils.

> ". . . fossils have furnished, through their record of the evolution of life on this planet, an amazingly effective key to the relative positioning of strata, . . ." (H.D. Hedberg, *Bulletin of the Geological Society of America*, V. 72, April 1961, p. 499).

For true believers in evolution, it may be logical to date rocks this way, even when this requires devising a method for explaining how the sediments got out of order. Since, however, we do not observe evolution taking place today, one must ask how they can be so confident that evolution was true in the past. The "answer" is that the evolutionary history of life is revealed by the fossil record in the sedimentary rocks. Dr. Pierre P. Grassè who for 30 years held the Chair of Evolution at the Sorbonne in Paris, one of the world's leading universities, has noted this fact:

> "Naturalists must remember that the process of evolution is revealed only through fossil forms" (*Evolution of Living Organisms*, Academic Press, 1977, p. 4).

That is, ancient rocks contain fossils of organisms in an early stage of evolution; younger rocks contain fossils representing a more advanced stage of evolution. We "know," of course, which rocks are ancient because they are the ones on the bottom, with the younger ones on top. But, then, we have just noted there are many places where this order is reversed. We "know" they are reversed because of the evolutionary stages of their respective fossils.

Now, if one senses a feeling of dizziness at this point, it is because we are going in circles. Maybe it will help settle our queasiness if we find some actual physical evidence that these gigantic old rock blocks have really ridden up and over (over-thrust) the younger ones. We would expect to find, if this is the case, a tremendous amount of rock breakage (brecciation) and ground-up rock powder at the interface, along with deep grooves and scratches (striations) along the undersurface, and a general mixture of the upper and lower rocks along the thrust plane. Is this what is found?

Not usually. Usually the contact surface is sharp and well defined, with the older rocks on top of the younger, often with many "ages" missing in between.

> "The following observations about 'overthrusts' seem to have universal validity: 1. The contact is usually sharp and impressive in view of the great amount of displacement . . . . 5. Minor folding and faulting can usually be observed in both the thrust plate and the underlying rocks. The intensity of such deformations is normally comparatively weak, at least in view of the large displacements these thrust plates have undergone" (P.E. Gretener, *Bulletin of Canadian Petroleum Geology,* Vol. 25, 1977, p. 110).

It is true, of course, that some "overthrusts" do exhibit evidence of brecciation and other such indicators of relative movement. Does this not prove they are really overthrusts?

Not at all — at least not necessarily. Many types of movement may occur besides overthrusting.

> "Late deformations, particularly by normal faulting, are present in many thrust plates. They should be recognized for what they are: post-thrusting features completely unrelated to the emplacement of the thrust plates" (*Ibid.*).

Then what deformations can be identified with confidence as caused by the thrust itself? The author of the above says that "basal tongues" from the lower plate are often injected into the base of the overthrust plate, and that these sometimes merge together. Also secondary "splay" thrusts may be found.

But now suppose that all these physical phenomena — brecciation, rock power, striations, basal tongues, splay thrusts, etc., that a real overthrust would produce, are actually present, does this finally prove that the rocks have really been moved out of their original depositional order?

Of course not. Such phenomena merely prove that the upper block has moved somewhat with respect to the lower block. This is quite common, even with formations in the "correct" sedimentary order, due to the different physical properties and times of deposition of the two formations, and proves nothing whatever about overthrusting.

Admittedly, such phenomena do not *rule out* the possibility of overthrusting, as their absence might do. They are necessary, but not sufficient, conditions for overthrusting. More evidence is needed — notably, evidence of the "roots" from which the alleged thrust block was derived, along with evidence that its incredible journey was physically possible.

Are the sources of the overthrust plates usually discernible? Only rarely, and with much speculation. Furthermore, in most cases, there are not any genuine evidences of overthrusting at all.

> "Different lithological units, usually with stratigraphic separation measured in kilometers, are in juxtaposition along a sharp contact, often no more impressive than a bedding plane" (*Ibid.,* p. 111).

Why then could it not be a simple bedding plane? And how do geologists explain the tremendous forces and motions in the earth that can accomplish the remarkable feat of moving a gigantic mass of rock great distances up and over another great rock formation? Tremendous compressive forces and rock strengths must be generated, and tremendous frictional forces overcome, before such an operation could ever be accomplished. The mechanism of the phenomenon has always been mysterious, and some of the most competent geophysicists have said it was impossible.

In 1959, however, William Rubey and M. King Hubbert felt they had solved the problem, proposing that water trapped in the pores of the sediments as they were deposited gradually became so compressed with the accumulating overburden that they developed "geostatic" pressures, capable actually of *floating* the formation above into another location (*Bulletin of Geological Society of America,* Vol. 70, February 1959, pp. 115-166).

This suggestion was enthusiastically accepted by most geologists and, for nearly three decades, has been by far the most widely adopted solution to the overthrusting problem. However, I immediately pointed out serious difficulties with it (see *The Genesis Flood*, pp. 196-200), and these are now becoming generally recognized and admitted.

It is obvious, for example, that these very high pore pressures can be maintained only if (1) the pores in the rock section near the interface are inter-connected, so the pressure will be applied over the entire base of the floating slab; (2) the permeability of the cap rock is so low that it provides an effective seal against the water escaping under the high pressure gradient to which it is subjected.

This is a highly unlikely combination of circumstances, and some geologists realize this.

> "At high enough pressures and temperatures, plastic flow will certainly reduce pore space inter-connectivity. To be effective mechanically, pore space must be inter-connected pore space; it is not clear that this is always the case during metamorphism. . . . Our preliminary results suggest that the effective permeability of the upper plate must be on the order of 10^{-3} mD or less for gravity gliding to be feasible. Otherwise, the fluid will leak away from the zone of decollement before pore pressure can reach the levels needed for gravity gliding. Although *in situ* rock permeabilities are poorly known, the few existing measurements suggest that

> effective permeabilities as low as 10^{-3} mD
> are rare in the geologic column . . . ."
> (J.H. Willemin, P.L. Guth and K.V.
> Hodges, *Geology*, September 1980,
> p. 405).

But suppose that, in some cases, rocks such as shales and evaporites do have sufficiently low permeabilities to seal off the high pressure zone. Now the problem becomes one of rock strength — the pressures become so high as to fracture the rocks!

> ". . . when the pore fluid pressure
> exceeds the least compressive stress,
> fractures will form normal to that stress
> direction . . . we suggest that pore
> pressure may never get high enough to
> allow gravity gliding as envisaged by
> Hubbert and Rubey . . . ." (*Ibid.*, p. 406).

If fractures develop, of course, this increases the permeability and the water flows out, lowering the pressure and stalling any incipient flotation. Furthermore, it is simply inconceivable that these huge (often many miles long, wide and thick) slabs of rock could traverse the long distances necessary without fractures developing from other causes as well. There seems no way to avoid escape of pore water through at least some fractures. By Pascal's law, if the pressure is lowered at any point in a continuous water body, it must drop by the same amount throughout the entire body. The whole scenario seems impossible, hydraulically, over any significant distances.

> "We suspect that over the areas of large
> thrust sheets such as those in the
> Appalachians or the Western Cordillera,

effective permeabilities would have been
too large to allow gravity gliding, even
with shale or evaporite cap rocks" (P.L.
Guth, L.V. Hodges and J.H. Willemin,
Geological Society of America Bulletin,
July 1982, p. 611).

It thus begins to appear that overthrusting by
floating is impossible on any noteworthy scale.
But this is not quite the last resort of those who
must salvage the evolutionary order at all costs.

"Simple gravity gliding under the
influence of elevated pore pressure cannot explain the Heart Mountain fault. . . .
Pierce has suggested a catastrophic
genesis for the Heart Mountain
allochthon" (*Ibid.*).

William Pierce (*Clastic Dykes of Heart Mountain
Fault Breccia,* (U.S.G.S. Prof. Paper 1133, 1979,
25 pp.) has been studying the Heart Mountain
"over-thrust" (Paleozoic over Eocene) for many
years. Originally, he thought it was caused by
simple gravity sliding, but this proved impossible
mechanically. Then it was suggested that the
mechanism might have involved the Hubbert and
Rubey fluid-pressure concept. Now that he finds
that won't work either, he has invoked
catastrophism — and catastrophism with a
vengeance, postulating an *explosive* transplanta-
tion of the thurst blocks! Catastrophic events,
however, obviously can neither be observed in
process nor modeled in the laboratory.

"Catastrophic processes are beyond the
scope of this analysis" (*Ibid.*).

One can *believe* in catastrophic overthrusting if

his motivation to do so is sufficiently strong, of course. If evolutionists want to retain their cherished evolutionary sequences, therefore, they must do so only by faith in catastrophism. Floating rock formations won't float!

OTHER EVIDENCES OF THE FLOOD

In the Appendix to *The Genesis Record* (Baker, 1976, pp. 683-686), I have listed 100 evidences of the worldwide flood as recorded in the Bible. Of these, 64 are evidences taken from the Bible itself, with 36 based on geological or other scientific data. It is obviously impossible to expound all of these here, but many of them have been discussed in *The Genesis Flood* and other creationist writings listed in Appendix A.

One very obvious example is the recognized fact that the entire globe has been under water in the past. Even the highest mountains (Himalayas, Alps, Andes, etc.) are composed at least in part of sedimentary rocks containing marine fossils. Evolutionists don't interpret these as all belonging to the same submergence, of course, but they do acknowledge that all major mountain ranges have been uplifted near the very end of the so-called geological ages. Also, we have shown reason to believe that all the geological column is a unit, formed rapidly and continuously.

Another significant point is that coal and oil, which are the most important geological resources economically, and provide employment for more geologists than all other occupations combined, are increasingly being recognized as catastrophic in origin, not requiring long ages at all, as once believed. In fact, they can each be formed quite rapidly in the laboratory.

"A group at Argonne National Laboratory

near Chicago, Illinois recently uncovered
some clues as to the origin of coal. The
studies indicate that currently accepted
theories of the development of coal
probably are wrong. . . . The group
heated undecomposed lignin, the
substance that holds plant cells
together, in the presence of mont-
morillite, or illite clay. The process led to
simple coals, whose rank depended on
the length of exposure to the 300° F
temperature" ("Basic Coal Studies Refute
Current Theories of Formation," *Research
and Development*, February 1984, p. 92).

With tremendous quantities of plant material
uprooted and transported by the waters of the
Flood, and with the indicated clay materials
abundantly available, plus heat (Genesis men-
tions eruptions from the fountains of the great
deep), conditions were ideal for the formation of
tremendous quantities of coal. The same is true
for oil and gas.

"For six years, two Australian
researchers patiently watched over a set
of 1-gm samples of organic material
sealed inside stainless steel 'bombs.' The
samples were derived from brown coal
and a type of oil shale called torbanite.
Each week, the temperature of the
samples was increased by 1° C, gradually
heating the material from 100° to 400°
C. . . . The researchers found that after
four years a product 'indistinguishable
from a paraffinic crude oil' was
generated from the torbanite-derived
samples, while brown coal produced a

> 'wet natural gas' '' (*Science News*, Vol.
> 125, March 24, 1984, p. 187).

There are also more and more indications that
oil can be formed rapidly in nature.

> "Oceanic hot springs, the site of strange
> colonies of marine life, may also be a
> breeding ground for new sources of oil
> and gas, according to new findings from
> a research mission in the Gulf of
> California.
> Scientists say that the discovery, in the
> Guaymas basin off Baja California,
> indicates that petroleum may be rapidly
> produced in nature under the pressure-
> cooker environment of these deep-sea
> springs — in thousands of years, rather
> than millions" (*Copley News Service*,
> January 30, 1982).

Another very obvious evidence of the worldwide
Flood is the worldwide drying up of inland lakes
and seas, along with the evidence that all river
valleys once carried much larger quantities of
water and alluvium than they do now. The
Pleistocene Epoch, also known as the Ice Age, is
the most recent of the supposed geological ages
and, in the Flood model of geology, is usually
believe to have followed the Flood as one of its
after-effects. The Ice Age in higher latitudes was
accompanied by a Pluvial Age in lower latitudes,
a rainy period in which the great deserts of the
world were all well watered, many with towns and
extensive agricultural works, and there were
great lakes and deep-flowing rivers everywhere,
including regions now arid and barren.

Sir Fred Hoyle and Elizabeth Butler have written
a fascinating description of this period, which

they also attributed to a worldwide catastrophe (not, however, the Genesis Flood, but a sudden impact of cometary dust over the world as a comet swept by).

> "Acquisition by the upper atmosphere of some 10^{14} gm. of cometary dust would have major implications on the Earth's climate. Pluvial activity would increase dramatically as temperature differences between sea and land widened. Global distribution of precipitation would be controlled by the density of the dust in the atmosphere; for a partially reflective blanket, a fraction of solar energy would still reach ground level creating new climatic zones. The totally undecomposed state of the interiors of Siberian Mammoths and the curious distribution, often uphill, of erratic boulders point to unbelievably sudden and severe conditions at the onset and possibly end of a glacial period. We suggest that a reflective blanket of particles could promote such conditions" ("On the Effect of a Sudden Change in the Albedo of the Earth," "Astrophysics and Space Science, Vol. 60, 1979, p. 505).

With only slight change, this paragraph by two eminent astrophysicists could describe what would happen when the Earth's primeval vapor canopy (implied by the "waters above the firmament" of Genesis 1:6-8) suddenly condensed and precipitated. In fact, one possible cause of its precipitation could well be the Earth's passage through a cloud of cometary or meteoritic dust. Hoyle and Butler go on to describe other probable after-effects:

> "Streams and rivers would flow for a
> while in enormous abundance, and in-
> land lakes would fill to exceptionally
> high levels, as in fact they did. The con-
> currence of pluvial conditions with ice
> ages is another challenge to 'small
> cause' theories, since a slow cooling
> together of oceans and lands over a time
> scale of approximately 10^4 years would
> decrease evaporation and precipitation,
> which the known pluvial conditions
> clearly show to be wrong. . . . The mam-
> moths became extinct during the last ice
> age. . . . But if the ice came slowly, over
> a time-span of approximately 10^4 years,
> a slow migration to the south would not
> only be possible, but we think inevitable"
> (*Ibid.*, p. 508).

Sir Fred and Dr. Butler are surely correct in
repudiating the various slow-and-gradual theories
that have been proposed for the onset of the Ice
Age. The Genesis Flood, however, provides the only
fully satisfactory explanation. The worldwide
warm climate indicated in the rocks and fossils of
almost all the world's other "geological ages"
finds an eminently satisfactory explanation in the
greenhouse effect caused by the antediluvian
water vapor canopy, whose sudden precipitation
brought on the great Flood and, probably, the
immediately subsequent Ice Age and Pluvial Age.
For an extensive discussion of the scientific
evidence supporting the vapor canopy concept,
readers are referred to the book *The Genesis
Flood*, and, even more, to *The Waters Above*, by
Dr. Jody Dillow (Moody Press, 1981, 479 pp.).

There are many significant evidences of the Flood — the worldwide depths of water-laid sedimentary rocks, the worldwide fossil graveyards, the worldwide flood traditions, the evidences of rapid and contemporaneous deposition of the complete geological column, the worldwide remnants of former lakes and great rivers, and many, many others.

To the Bible-believing Christian, however, the greatest and conclusive evidence is that it is clearly taught in the Word of God. According to the Genesis record, the waters covered the highest mountains of the world for at least a year, destroying all living creatures of the dry land. Preservation of life was accomplished only by Noah's gigantic Ark, whose construction would have been ridiculously unnecessary for only a local flood (the supposition, by some Christian geologists that the Flood was global but "tranquil" (!) is merely a commentary on their ignorance of both hydraulics and Scripture).

Furthermore, these Old Testament descriptions of the worldwide hydraulic cataclysm are confirmed by Christ and the Apostles in the New Testament. The Christian, therefore, has no *legitimate* option to accepting such a cataclysm, rather than the evolutionary geological ages, as the basic framework within which to interpret all the geological and other physical remnants of the Earth's primeval history.

The great rocks and fossil beds of the earth, therefore, are not in any way evidence of evolution, as widely believed. Instead, they constitute sort of a gigantic tombstone, describing the violent demise of the "world that then was" (II Peter 3:6), recording the judgment of a righteous God on a rebellious Earth.

Thus, everywhere we look in the earth, we see a great stone testimony that God still rules His world, and judges sin. Instead of being an embarrassment to Christians, forcing them into a compromise with evolutionists and their vaunted geological ages, these rock beds and fossil graveyards offer a tremendous tool for witnessing, showing people that the Bible record is true and that the great Flood is, as Christ Himself said, a type and promise of His coming again to judge an unbelieving sinful world, and to deliver all His redeemed ones from that world, receiving them into His presence forever.

Appendix A

ANNOTATED BIBLIOGRAPHY OF KEY CREATIONIST BOOKS

Each of the books listed below will provide further help and information on one or more of the topics surveyed in this book. Since creationist literature has become quite extensive in recent years, the list is necessarily selective rather than complete, but it is representative and should meet all relevant needs. Many of the books listed have been greatly used in furthering the modern revival of creationism, and readers are urged to obtain and study as many of them as possible. They can be ordered either through local Christian book stores or direct from the indicated publishers. Also, if preferred, any book in this annotated bibliography can be ordered through the Institute for Creation Research, P.O. Box 2667, El Cajon, California 92021. (Phone: (619) 440-2443).

* * * * * * * * * *

Austin, Steven, *Catastrophes in Earth History* (Institute for Creation Research, 1984, 318 pp.). Extensive annotated and analytical bibliography of modern secular geological books and papers supporting catastrophism.

Aw, S.E., *Chemical Evolution: An Examination of Current Ideas* (Creation-Life Publishers, 1982, 206 pp.). A careful scientific critique of naturalistic theories of the biochemical origin of life.

Bliss, Richard B., Duane T. Gish and Gary E. Parker, *Fossils: Key to the Present* (Institute for Creation Research, 1980, 80 pp.). A strikingly illustrated study on the significance of the fossil record, easily understood and written from a scientific two-model approach.

Bliss, Richard B. and Gary E. Parker, *Origin of Life* (Institute for Creation Research, 1979, 70 pp.). A beautifully illustrated and simple discussion of the origin of life, written with a scientific two-model approach.

Bowden, Malcolm, *Ape-Men: Fact or Fallacy* (Sovereign Publications, England, 1977, 258 pp.). Critical analysis of the supposed fossil evidence for ape-men intermediates, demonstrating that there is no valid evidence that humans evolved from any ape-like ancestor.

Bowden, Malcolm, *The Rise of the Evolution Fraud* (Creation-Life Publishers, 1982, 277 pp.). The history and rise to prominence of the theory of evolution through Lyell, Darwin and others in 19th Century England, stressing the ultimate anti-Christian goals of the movement.

DeYoung, Donald B. and John C. Whitcomb, *The Moon: Its Creation, Form and Significance* (BMH Books, 1978, 180 pp.). Well-documented discussion of the nature of the moon and its origin by special, recent creation, with numerous illustrations and photographs.

Dillow, Joseph C., *The Waters Above* (Moody Press, 1981, 479 pp.). Detailed exposition of the Biblical and scientific evidence for the world's vapor canopy before the great flood.

Gish, Duane T., *Dinosaurs - Those Terrible Lizards* (Creation-Life Publishers, 1977, 62 pp.). A dramatically illustrated book about dinosaurs written from the Biblical, creationist point of view, and suitable for all ages. Also includes the fascinating story of the bombardier beetle, with its possible implications for tales of fire-breathing dragons.

Gish, Duane T., *Evolution: The Challenge of the Fossil Record*, Master Books, 1985, 277 pp.). The most complete and cogent treatment available on the key fossil evidence related to origins and earth history.

Gish, Duane T., *Speculations and Experiments on the Origin of Life: A Critique* (Institute for Creation Research, 1972, 41 pp.). An analysis and devasting critique of current theories and laboratory experiments attempting to support a naturalistic development of life from non-living chemicals.

Lubenow, Marvin, *From Fish to Gish* (Creation-Life Publishers, 1983, 304 pp.). A fascinating volume summarizing and analyzing most of the creation-evolution debates in which ICR scientists have participated.

Moore, John N., How to Teach Origins without ACLU Interference (Mott Media, 1983, 382 pp.). A comprehensive treatment of content and method suitable for teaching creation and evolution on a two-model basis in public schools, written by a science professor who successfully taught such a course for many years in a large state university.

Morris, Henry M., *The Biblical Basis for Modern Science* (Baker Book House, 1984, 500 pp.). A comprehensive textbook or general reference book on science and Scripture. Each of 12 major fields of science, with corresponding Biblical principles and insights, is covered in a separate chapter, in addition to four introductory chapters on theology, cosmology, miracles and evolutionism. Well documented and illustrated, with many useful appendixes, complete bibliographies and indexes.

Morris, Henry M., *Education for the Real World* (Creation-Life Publishers, 1983, 285 pp.). A widely used textbook on the Biblical doctrine of education, documenting the damaging impact of evolutionary humanism in the schools and stressing the foundational importance of creationism in true education.

Morris, Henry M., *Evolution in Turmoil* (Creation-Life Publishers, 1982, 190 pp.). Documented account of current conflicts within evolutionism and the impact of creationism on the humanistic establishment in science and education.

Morris, Henry M., *The Genesis Record* (Baker Book House, 1976, 716 pp.). A complete verse-by-verse commentary on Genesis, with emphasis on the scientific implications of its early chapters and with thorough treatment of all problem passages, in an easily understood narrative exposition. Over 60,000 copies sold.

Morris, Henry M., *History of Modern Creationism* (Master Books, 1984, 382 pp.). The only complete history of the modern creationist movement, with introductory chapters covering the creation/evolution conflict throughout earlier times as well, and with an assessment of the current situation and future developments. Parts of the book are autobiographical.

Morris, Henry M., *King of Creation* (Creation-Life Publishers, 1980, 239 pp.). The modern creation movement placed in Biblical perspective, emphasizing Christ as Creator and Sovereign. Well-documented evidence of the scientific strength and spiritual impact of creationism. Foreword by Josh McDowell.

Morris, Henry M., *Many Infallible Proofs* (Creation-Life Publishers, 1974, 381 pp.). A comprehensive and systematic survey of the overwhelming evidences for the inerrant inspiration of the Bible and the unique truth and authority of Christianity.

Morris, Henry M., *Men of Science - Men of God* (Creation-Life Publishers, 1982, 128 pp.). Brief biographies of 62 great Bible-believing scientists of the past, including most of the "founding fathers" of modern science, refuting the modern allegation that true scientists cannot be Christian creationists.

Morris, Henry M., *Scientific Creationism* (2nd Edition Creation-Life Publishers, 1985, 308 pp.). The most widely used general text and reference book on scientific creationism, showing clearly the superiority of the creation model of origins to the evolution model. Comprehensive and thoroughly documented.

Morris, Henry M., *The Troubled Waters of Evolution* (Creation-Life Publishers, 1974, 217 pp.). The most complete account, from a Biblical and creationist point of view, of the long history and pervasive and deadly influence of evolutionary thought.

Morris, John D., *Tracking those Incredible Dinosaurs - and the People Who Knew Them* (Creation-Life Publishers, 1980, 240 pp.). The complete record and geological analysis of the famous human and dinosaur footprints in the limestone beds of the Paluxy River in Texas. Extensively illustrated evidences of the contemporaneity of man and dinosaurs.

Parker, Gary E., and Henry M. Morris, *What is Creation Science?* (Creation-Life Publishers, 1982, 306 pp.). A scientific defense of creation, with no Biblical or theological material. Well illustrated and fully documented.

Rendle-Short, John, *Man: Ape or Image?* (Master Books, 1981, 195 pp.). Biblical, theological and scientific evidences supporting the doctrine of man as a special creation of God.

Slusher, Harold S., *Age of the Cosmos* (Institute for Creation Research, 1980, 76 pp.). A technical study of the many evidences in astronomy, cosmology and other sciences indicating a recent creation of the cosmos.

Slusher, Harold S., *Critique of Radiometric Dating* (Institute for Creation Research, 1981, 58 pp.). Evaluation and refutation, from sound principles of physics, of the most important radiometric methods of determining geologic ages.

Slusher, Harold S., *Origin of the Universe* (Institute for Creation Research, 1980, 90 pp.). Technical monograph indicating the fatal falacies of the Big-Bang and Steady-State cosmogonies.

Whitcomb, John C., The Early Earth (Presbyterian and Reformed Publ. Co., 1972, 144 pp.). Analysis of the Biblical evidence for recent creation and a worldwide flood, with critique of the gap theory and other attempts to harmonize Genesis with uniformitarianism.

Whitcomb, John C., and Henry M. Morris, *The Genesis Flood* (Presbyterian and Reformed Publ. Co., 1961, 518 pp.). The most comprehensive exposition of the Biblical and scientific evidences of the great Flood and related events in earth history. Thoroughly documented and indexed, this was the definitive work which catalyzed the modern revival of creationism.

Whitcomb, John C., *The World that Perished* (Baker Book House, 1973, 155 pp.). A brief sequel to *The Genesis Flood* by one of its co-authors, with answers to published critical reviews of the book and with additional evidences supporting the Biblical record.

Wilder-Smith, A.E., *Man's Origin, Man's Destiny* (Creation-Life Publishers, 1968, 320 pp.). A comprehensive study of the scientific evidence for creation in light of Scripture, by an outstanding European scientist.

Wysong, R.L. *The Creation-Evolution Controversy* (Inquiry Publishing Co., 1976, 455 pp.). One of the most comprehensive treatments of the scientific evidences relating to origins. Well illustrated, objective treatment.

Appendix B

CREATIONIST PERIODICALS

The concerned Christian should keep abreast of new developments in the creationist revival, as well as new creationist books, by taking one or more of the following periodicals. Although an increasing number of other periodicals are now available, these are probably the most influential and widely read.

* * * * * * * * * *

Acts and Facts. Monthly newsletter for the Institute for Creation Reserach, including a special "Impact" article each month. Subscriptions free on request to Institute for Creation Research, P.O. Box 2667, El Cajon, California 92021.

Bible-Science Newsletter. Monthly newsletter of the Bible-Science Association. For membership and subscription information, write to B.S.A., 2911 E. 42nd Street, Minneapolis, Minnesota, 55406.

Creation Research Society Quarterly. Journal of research papers in scientific and Biblical creationism. For membership application or subscription information, write to Creation Research Society, 2717 Cranbrook Rd., Ann Arbor, Michigan, 48104.

Creation Social Science and Humanities Quarterly. Journal of scholarly papers written from the creationist perspective in the humanities and the social sciences. For membership application or subscription information, write the Creation Social Science and Humanities Society, 1429 N. Holyoke, Wichita, Kansas, 67208.

Ex Nihilo. Monthly magazine published by the Creation-Science Foundation of Australia. Subscriptions may be placed through the C.S.F. American Office at C.S.F., P.O. Box 18339, Tucson, Arizona, 85731.

Appendix C

Creation Books and Videos

There are many creationist books and videos available from Master Books. They are valuable, not only for your own enjoyment and education, but for use in churches, schools and home Bible-studies.

The materials range from wonderful children's books, to highly technical monographs by leading creation scientists. The majority of books are written in easy-to-understand language that makes learning about God's creation a pleasure.

Videos range from children's videos, single topic videos, to a complete creation seminar (10 tapes), "Understanding Genesis."

For a complete catalog of Master Books products write or call:

Master Books
P.O. Box 1606
El Cajon, CA 92022
Phone (619) 448-1121

Index of Names

Index of Subjects

S

Index of Scriptures